# FUN FOODS

## Clever Ideas for Garnishing & Decorating

## Wim Kros

Sterling Publishing Co., Inc.  New York

# Acknowledgments

The author wishes to acknowledge Margot with extra thanks. Without her support this book could not have been realized.

Translation edited by
Rodman Neumann

Translation and adaptation:
TDS/Utrecht, The Netherlands;
Tony Burrett

Editorial:
Margot Kros-Maas
Martha Regtering-Maassen (pg. 16–31)
Mario en Martien van Herpen (pg. 37–43, 97, 113)
Anneke v.d. Molen (pg. 100–103)

Design:
Wim Kros/Cees Overvoorde

Photography:
Wim Kros

**Library of Congress Cataloging-in-Publication Data**

Kros, Wim.
   [Sierlijk smullen. English]
   Fun foods : clever ideas for garnishing & decorating / by Wim Kros.
      p.    cm.
   Translation of: Sierlijk smullen.
   ISBN 0-8069-7280-7.—ISBN 0-8069-7281-5 (pbk.)
   1. Garnishes (Cookery)  2. Food presentation.  3. Cake decorating.
 I. Title.
TX740.5.K7613   1990
641.8′1—dc20
                                             89-26284
                                                 CIP

English translation copyright © 1990 by
Sterling Publishing Co., Inc.
387 Park Avenue South, New York, N.Y. 10016
Original edition published in The Netherlands
under the title "Sierlijk smullen, garneren
en dekoreren van eten, hapjes en ander lekkers"
© 1987 by B. V. Uitgeversmaatschappij Tirion, Baarn
Distributed in Canada by Sterling Publishing
% Canadian Manda Group, P.O. Box 920, Station U
Toronto, Ontario, Canada M8Z 5P9
Distributed in Great Britain and Europe by Cassell PLC
Artillery House, Artillery Row, London SW1P 1RT, England
Distributed in Australia by Capricorn Ltd.
P.O. Box 665, Lane Cove, NSW 2066
*Printed and bound in Hong Kong*

# Contents

# Introduction

On festive occasions, or when we have something special to celebrate, we usually make a little extra effort, paying more attention to our appearance and the way we dress. Moreover, we often devote extra attention to the environment in which the celebration will take place; we hang up decorations, adorn a Christmas tree, bedeck an Easter or Thanksgiving table. In short, we try to create a jolly and festive atmosphere. Of course, we also make an extra effort concerning the food we serve on these occasions, and that is what this book is all about.

This is not an exclusive cookbook full of exotic new recipes, but a relatively simple "do-it-yourself" book, with straightforward instructions and, where necessary, simple recipes, to enable you to transform ordinary everyday dishes — slices of cake, rolls and sandwiches, desserts and salads — into fun foods — festive and mouth-watering feasts!

One important difference between this and many other "cookbooks" is that wide use is made of working photographs so that you can see how the work progresses step by step. We advise you to study these photographs carefully and to read the text thoroughly before you begin work. If you do this, then success is almost guaranteed, whether you are a beginner or an experienced cook.

The most important thing is to allow your imagination to run free and to have lots of fun while you are preparing the fun food described here. Of course, the knowledge that your creations, prepared with such love and skill, will quickly disappear into the tummies of your family and friends, is a little frustrating — but try to think of it as the compliment that it undoubtedly is!

We wish you success and bon appétit!

Wim Kros.

# Materials and utensils, your work area, and basic recipes

◄ Besides everyday materials — the sorts of things probably already in your kitchen cupboards — you will need the following items:

○ waxed paper
○ aluminum foil
○ transparent tracing paper or sandwich wrapping paper
○ thin cardboard or sturdy drawing paper
○ toothpicks
○ miniature flags and parasols
○ aluminum trays
○ cookie cutters
○ adhesive tape

▲ If you don't have a good supply of confectioners' sugar on hand, it is hardly worth reading further! Buy a large quantity, at least 2 lb (1 kilo), at a time. This is more economical than buying a smaller box.

▼ Lacy paper doilies (see below) are almost indispensable for a presentation that is decorative and stylish, and for serving or wrapping the fun foods described in this book. Most finer department stores stock a wide variety. They range in size from 4 to 12 in (10 to 30 cm) in diameter, and from 6 × 9 in (15 × 24 cm) to 8 × 16 in (20 × 40 cm) in rectangular forms. They come in white and various other colors, including gold and silver.

Department stores also stock a variety of edible decorations — flowers, animals, all kinds of imaginative and fanciful shapes, etc. Extracts and flavorings can also be found in these stores. ▶

Food coloring, which ▲ meets consumer protection regulations, can be found in most large stores that specialize in household and kitchen items, and often at supermarkets.

◄ Baking powders, cake mixes, glazes, nuts, decorative sugar work, and all the other items you need can be found in most supermarkets. At any time you will want to have lots and lots of sugar confetti, candy flowers, and chocolate buttons as part of the basic stock in your cupboard.

The everyday tools and ▶ utensils that you will need to prepare all the fun foods described here won't be mentioned separately. But those that are so allied to a specific product or technique that it is impossible to class them as basic equipment are described in the text where necessary.

We also won't describe standard kitchen equipment (mixer, kitchen knives, bowls, etc.), because these tools and utensils can be found in almost any household.

Basic equipment which you must have includes:

○ icing turntable
○ hot plate
○ piping bag(s)
○ adaptor(s)
○ decorating tubes (nozzles)
○ garnishing knives
○ tweezers
○ utility knife
○ narrow, flat pastry brushes of hog's hair

A piping bag with an ▶ adaptor and decorating tube or nozzle can, in some cases, especially in incidental use, be replaced by plastic squeeze bottles. These can be obtained at do-it-yourself and hobby stores where they are sold for silk painting and other uses. A paper cone (see page 10) also serves the purpose.

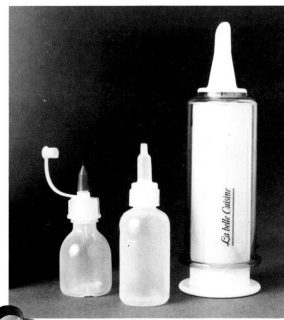

Specialty shops often stock unusual, highly specific and beautiful kitchen utensils. Browsing through a store such as this is always worthwhile, even if you don't actually buy anything. What you will come away with is lots of information and many ideas.▼

◀ You can never have enough cookie cutters! Make sure that you have as varied an assortment as possible; not only in shape but also in size.

9

## YOUR WORK AREA

Most of the preparation, such as readying the ingredients, cooking or baking, and so forth, is carried out in the kitchen.

In many cases, decorative work can be done on the kitchen counter as well, but in practice sitting at a table is much more pleasant. Decoration can take a lot of time — standing in an immobile, slightly bent position is very tiring — and as well, when you are sitting down, your work is nearer your eye level. This is certainly true when you are using an icing turntable, which even improves your overall view of the piece you are working on.

Moreover, if you sit at a table when you work, your arms and hands have adequate support for fine decorative work. This is not the case when you stand at the kitchen counter.

Thus, it is best to sit at the dining room table, a desk, or some similar surface when

you are engaged in this type of work. Cover the surface with a smooth, stiff, plastic tablecloth.

Proper lighting is very important, particularly for such fine work as piping flowers, decorating cookies, incising rind or peel, etc. The best combination is an overhead neon light with an incandescent lamp that is adjustable near the work.

Make sure that you have enough wooden chopping boards, smaller boards, and trays. If you already do, or expect to do, decoration and garnishing often, then try to keep the special utensils and materials together for easy use. A separate, easily removable drawer, a small portable (filing) cabinet, or a special chest or box are perfect for keeping these items. Store your bought or homemade decorative candy and other supplies in stackable, compartmented, plastic boxes (see photo above). After a while, you will have a good assortment, and you will have your own reasons why it is vital to keep these supplies in some kind of order. Nothing is more aggravating than not being able to lay your hands on a particular item you need when meanwhile the icing is drying!

Before you begin: set out **everything** you need on, or near, your working surface. With proper preparation you can work undisturbed, with the minimum distraction — and that can only benefit the end result!

### Oven Temperatures

| | | | | |
|---|---|---|---|---|
| 285°F | — | 140°C | — | Mark 1 |
| 320°F | — | 160°C | — | Mark 2 |
| 360°F | — | 180°C | — | Mark 3 |
| 390°F | — | 200°C | — | Mark 4 |
| 430°F | — | 220°C | — | Mark 5 |
| 465°F | — | 240°C | — | Mark 6 |
| 500°F | — | 260°C | — | Mark 7 |
| 535°F | — | 280°C | — | Mark 8 |

If you do not have a ▶ piping bag with an adaptor and a fine decorating tube, you can use a paper cone or cornet to pipe lines of various thicknesses. For this you need a sheet of waxed or baking paper about 7 × 12 in (18 × 30 cm). Cut this sheet in half diagonally. If you are right-handed, lay the sheet on your work surface so that the right angle is to the top left and the more acute-angled point is towards you. Mark an *X* on the upper side of the paper halfway along the diagonal edge and another on the back side of the right angle (see photo 1). Fold the right-angled corner inward so that the marks lie one on top of the other, and hold these in place between the thumb and fingers of the right hand. Take the lower, more acute-angled point in the left hand (see photo 2).

Fold this point over and twist it around until a cone is formed. The cone should have a sharp point at one end and a fairly wide opening at the other (see photo 3). Now fold the narrow point, which you are holding in your left hand, over the edge towards the inside of the cone (see photo 4), and your cone is almost ready for use. Cut off the point to make an opening of the width you require, and fill the cone with icing or cream. Now fold or roll the paper over to close the wide opening. Squeeze out the icing, folding the top over as you do so, with steady pressure until the cone is empty (see photo 5). ▶

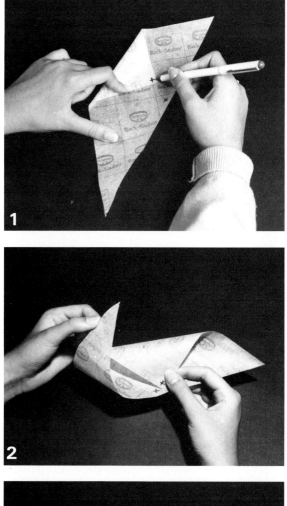

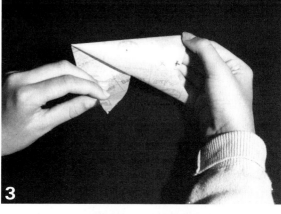

## Basic recipe for water icing

**Preparation:** Sieve the sugar, and blend it with the hot water and other ingredients in an electric mixer. Add the water slowly. Continue to blend until the icing has a beautiful glaze. Make sure that it is not too thin; otherwise it will tend to "flow." It should be liquid but thick in texture; it may not be necessary to use all the water. If you are piping (line) figures, then add less water. If the icing becomes too thick, then, after pouring, smooth it out with a knife dipped in hot water.

This type of icing is rather transparent. It remains soft, even after it has "dried," much longer than does icing made with egg white and is therefore preferable to egg-white icing, especially for cake and cookies. However, it is less suitable for use as a mortar in fixing decorations.

### INGREDIENTS

- 8 oz (250 g) confectioners' sugar
- 2 to 3 Tbs hot water
- food coloring
- lemon juice (to make the icing less sweet) or
- flavoring (extract, liqueur, etc.)

## Basic recipe for egg-white icing

**Preparation:** Beat the egg whites in a mixer until they are stiff; then add the sieved confectioners' sugar, a spoonful at a time. Ensure that no egg yolk gets into the mixture. Halfway through this operation add the lemon juice or flavoring and the food coloring. Continue to add sugar (and, if necessary, food coloring) until indentations made in the icing with a knife remain. It is now suitable for piping decorative borders, flower petals, etc. If the icing is used to ice a cake or tart, make it a little thinner by not adding as much sugar. Work the icing at room temperature, but store it in a closed container in the refrigerator. Piped icing is left to "dry" in the open air and will become very hard after a day or two. Egg-white icing is particularly suitable for use as mortar to fix "hard" foodstuffs that do not contain moisture (cake, confectionery, etc.). Never leave your egg-white icing work in a damp place or humid atmosphere.

### INGREDIENTS

- 2 egg whites from medium-sized eggs
- 10 to 13 oz (300 to 400 g) confectioners' sugar
- lemon juice or flavoring (extract)
- food coloring

## Basic recipe for butter cream

Take the butter out of the refrigerator about a half hour beforehand. Beat it in a mixer until it is creamy. Continue to beat, adding the flavoring and sieved confectioners' sugar. If necessary, leave the butter cream to stiffen for a while in the refrigerator. Butter cream can either be spread or piped, but it remains very soft and can only be kept for a limited period of time.

### INGREDIENTS

- 7 oz (200 g) butter
- 3½ oz (100 g) confectioners' sugar
- flavoring (liqueur, vanilla sugar, chocolate, extract, etc.)

# Sugar cubes as decorative reliefs and for three-dimensional figures

This festive presentation of sugar cubes in the form of a polar landscape, or some similar design, is perfect for a large party or reception, such as a holiday celebration, a wedding, or a birthday party. The human and animal figures are built of cubes fixed together with *sugar mortar*. For solid, rectangular buildings or sugar cubes, mortar is not always necessary provided you stagger the cubes the way bricks are laid — so that the cubes lock each other in place. For round shapes, or those that slope inward (roofs for example), the cubes must be attached with mortar. A tiny drop is all you need so that the cubes will break off easily. The cubes in the arrangement are, after all, meant to sweeten tea or coffee!

Although it perhaps is not obvious at first, there is no reason why sugar cubes cannot be presented in much the same way as cookies or candy. These are typically served nicely arranged on a plate or a tray, but commonly sugar cubes are put in a bowl or a serving dish without any thought to their

A sugar cube relief is rather more "sober" in appearance and is therefore more suitable for a business meeting, a more serious reception, or perhaps a coffee hour with friends. Do not forget to lay out a pair of sugar tongs.

The cubes on the left are laid out loose in a serving dish; those in the reliefs on the opposite page are fixed together with a tiny drop of mortar. ▶

12

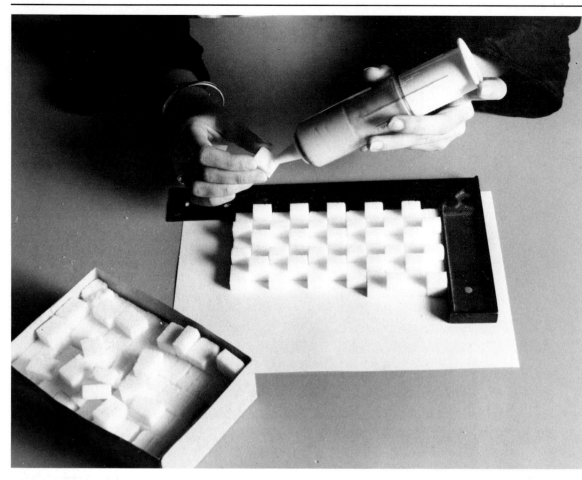

## RELIEFS

◄ The easiest way to build a relief is to use a metal try square (see photo, left) and work on waxed paper. Always make a test pattern from loose cubes first. Remember that patterns in which the cubes are set at angles will also have an irregular outline (see page 13). Design a pattern in which, as far as possible, the cubes fit together at right angles. Remember that a sugar cube has three different sides and can be positioned in six different ways. Each cube should be contacted on all sides so that there are no gaps between cubes. If you are not fixing your relief with sugar paste, use a tray with vertical edges for the arranging.

arrangement. When serving tea or coffee to guests, the host often simply places the box of cubes on the table saying "Help yourself to sugar"! But there is a much better and more creative way of doing this — as you can see in the photographs on these pages. Geometrical reliefs, for example, can be built up within the rim of a serving tray into a variety of interesting patterns. An even more creative approach is to build an Eskimo igloo, together with a few "Eskimos" and huskies. The white sugar cubes are perfect for this, and the "icy" effect can be heightened by sprinkling the outside with confectioners' sugar.

When fixing the cubes ► together, always use as little mortar as possible. This not only applies to the igloo, but also particularly to the reliefs.

If you use the mortar too generously, it squeezes out between the cubes and spoils the appearance of the finished work. Moreover, this makes the cubes more difficult to break off.

## IGLOO INSTRUCTIONS

Using a compass, draw a circle of radius 3.5 in (9 cm) on a sheet of white paper. The first row of cubes is placed **inside** the circumference of this circle just drawn. You need 17 cubes to form the open circle and 4 cubes, 2 on each side at right angles, to form the entrance. The entrance cubes thus protrude beyond the circle. Now lay the second layer, working alternately left and right from the entrance towards the back of the igloo. Because the circles decrease in size, you may not be able to finish the circles with whole cubes. Each layer is

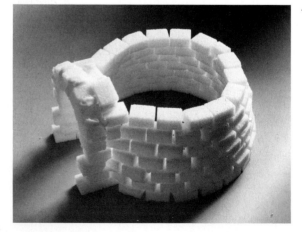

◄ The igloo consists of approximately 200 sugar cubes, is 6 in (14.5 cm) in height (12 layers of cubes), and has an outer diameter of 7¼ in (18 cm). The base layer is a partial circle of 21 cubes: 17 in the circle with 2 on either side to form the entrance. The inner width of the base of the entrance is 2½ in (6 cm).

closed at the back by setting the last cube at a right angle jutting inward or by placing a cube broken between your fingers that just fits the gap. Only use sugar paste to fill in as a last resort. Make sure that you stagger the cubes the way a builder lays bricks.

Apply a daub of sugar paste to only the cube you are working with — not the cubes already laid. As the circles get smaller with the increasing height of the igloo, the work goes quicker since there are fewer cubes to lay! After every three or four layers, set the igloo aside for at least 8 hours to allow the sugar paste to dry and

Both the Eskimos and▲ the huskies are built in stages. These are, for the Eskimos, feet and legs, arms and body, and head and hat. Glue together each part and allow to dry for 24 hours. Then assemble the parts.

A similar method is used for some parts of the igloo: the arch above the entrance and the upper circle(s) of the roof, for ◄example.

## EQUIPMENT

○ metal try square
○ large sheet of white bond paper
○ square or rectangular tray with vertical sides
○ ruler and pencil
○ compass
○ piping bag or squeeze bottle
○ icing turntable — this is not absolutely necessary but it does simplify the work of building with sugar cubes.

## INGREDIENTS

○ Sugar cubes in a 2 lb (1 kilo) box, approximately 375 cubes. Only use good undamaged examples with straight edges for building your reliefs and models.
○ egg white
○ confectioners' sugar

harden. Do not apply pressure to the assembled layers until the paste has had at least 24 hours to harden. Some details — the arch over the entrance, for example, and the last flat part of the roof — must be built separately. (See the photograph above.) Make these on a separate sheet of paper; allow the sugar paste to harden, and then add them to the igloo. You can remove irregular projections and any excess paste by dissolving them with a wetted finger. The finished igloo, along with the accompanying Eskimos and huskies, is served on a large dish. To give the effect of snow, sprinkle with granulated sugar.

# Decorative borders and flowers made of icing

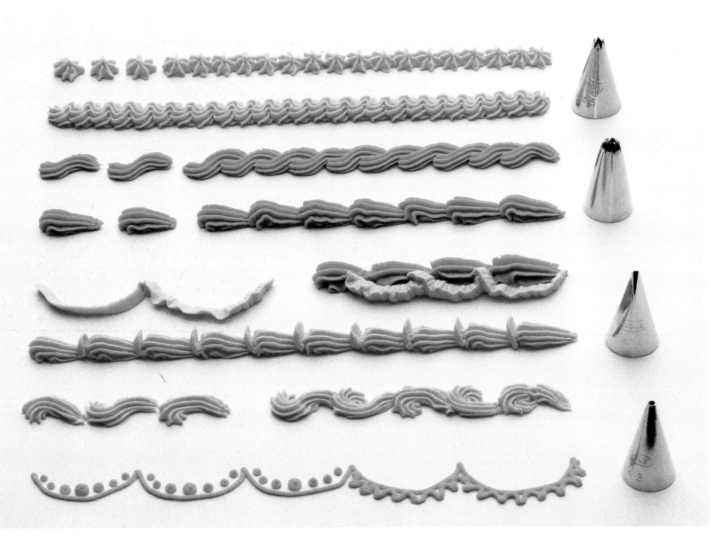

The application of an egg-white icing (or some other icing) to cakes, pastries, cookies, etc. is commonly referred to simply as "icing." Icing can be applied flat (with a spatula) or in relief (using shaped tubes or nozzles which fit into a piping bag). A flat, smooth layer of icing is usually enlivened with piped edges, flowers, or some other form of decoration.

Icing is a mixture of sieved confectioners' sugar, egg whites, lemon juice, and food coloring. After 12 to 24 hours icing that has been piped or spread is thoroughly hardened. In its original state, this type of icing is already fairly stiff and is therefore suitable for making three-dimensional

▲ These decorative borders are for tarts, cakes, and cookies and are piped with egg-white icing. This fully hardens after 6 to 24 hours. The icing will remain much softer if, after a few hours, you cover the cake with a clean, damp dish towel.

If you prefer very soft confectionery, then you can use water icing to cover the cake itself and soft butter cream (see pages 10/11) for the decoration.

## HALF ROSE

See the instructions on page 23.
Petal motif Ateco 103 (UK 42);
Lettering motif Ateco 4 (UK 3).

**U.K. No 42**

**U.K. No 3**

## WHOLE ROSE

See the instructions on page 24.
Petal motif Ateco 103 (UK 42);
Lettering motif Ateco 4 (UK 3).

**U.K. No 42**

**U.K. No 3**

## YELLOW DAFFODIL

See the instructions on page 23.
Petal motif Ateco 61 (UK 18);
Lettering motif Ateco 2 (UK 2).

**U.K. No 18**

**U.K. No 2**

## POPPY

See the instructions on page 23.
Petal motif Ateco 102 (UK 11);
Lettering motif Ateco 2 (UK 2).

**U.K. No 11**

**U.K. No 2**

In order to make decorative borders and flowers from egg-white icing the following equipment is necessary (numbers correspond to photo, left):

○ plastic containers with lids
○ piping bag(s) (1)
○ adaptor(s) (4)
○ tubes (nozzles) (2)
○ hand mixer
○ spoons
○ baking paper or waxed paper
○ garnishing plate, 12 by 16 in (30 by 40 cm). (Use an acrylic cutting board or a thin laminated board.)
○ paper towels
○ spatula (5)
○ icing turntable (6)
○ aluminum foil
○ pastry brush (7)
○ icing nails (8)

## INGREDIENTS

○ egg whites
○ sieved confectioners' sugar
○ lemon juice
○ food coloring

Because of the large quantity of powdered sugar it contains, egg-white icing is very sweet. Those who prefer their icing less sweet can add a little lemon juice or a few drops of flavoring extract to the basic mixture.

shapes. The flower shapes on page 17 are a good example of this. Egg-white icing, however, is less commonly used as a finish for many cakes, cookies, and tarts, because most people prefer the much softer water icing (confectioners' sugar and water) to the harder icing made with egg whites. Egg-white icing is mostly used for decoration and sometimes as a finish to small, flat tarts which can be bought in specialty shops — see also pages 88 and 92.

Icing made from confectioners' sugar and either egg whites or water are both generally known as icing (as in their application, mentioned above) and also as frosting. In this chapter we use the word "icing" to refer only to egg-white icing and not to water icing — which is really too soft for our purposes. (See also pages 10 and 11.)

In the following pages we will cover these subjects:
A. The piping of various decorative edges, borders, and lines on the top or sides of cakes, tarts, and cookies.
B. The piping of a layer of icing in relief on tarts and cakes as shown in the photographs of the Volkswagen and the snowman on pages 20 and 21. For this type of work, pattern No. 1 — the drop-flower pattern — typically is used.
C. The piping of three-dimensional flowers and similar shapes.
D. The application of a smooth layer of icing. The cake with roses shown on page 25 was made using a combination of techniques A, C, and D.
E. The making of candy dolls (for decorating children's birthday cakes, among other things) from peppermint sticks, balls of chewing gum, and icing.

But first here are the 8 most important decorative borders, which you can easily alter and/or amplify to suit your own taste. To make these borders you need only four tubes (or nozzles) — **Ateco numbers 4, 17, 102, 31** (UK 3, 5, 11, and 27).

Each border is built up by constantly repeating a particular basic figure. First practise this figure separately on a sheet of waxed paper. Once you are able to pipe a series of figures that are exactly alike (same shape, same size), only then are you ready to begin decorating your work. The figures should be piped close together (or even overlapping) so that a continuous, unbroken border is formed.

## 1. DROP-FLOWER BORDER

For this pretty, easy-to-make border you need Ateco tube 17 (UK 5). The icing must be fairly stiff, or the flowers will not hold their shape. Allow the tube to rest on the piece of work and hold the piping bag upright.

To make an open flower, squeeze evenly; then stop, and lift the piping bag away. To make a "spun" flower, first twist the hand holding the piping bag as far as possible to the left. Then, as you squeeze out the icing, untwist your hand completely to the right; stop, and lift the bag away. Make sure that the flowers are the same size and that the distances between them are the same.

## 2. ZIGZAG BORDER

In principle the zigzag border is made in a single uninterrupted movement, using Ateco tube 17 (UK 5).

Hold the piping bag at the "three o'clock" position and at an angle of 45°. Set the mouth of the decorating tube on the surface of the work. Make short, up-and-down movements so that the zigzag actually forms a straight line. Both the pressure you apply and the movement must be as even and regular as possible.

## 3. TWISTED-CORD BORDER

This decorative border is somewhat more difficult to make than the previous two. Use Ateco tube 17 (UK 5) to begin; if you require a wider border, use Ateco tube 16, 30, or 31 (UK 7, 14, or 27). Begin by piping a half circle — rather like the arch of an eyebrow. Now position the tube under this arch, and pipe an extended S-shape. Repeat this continuously. Try to make the "S" shapes as alike as possible.

## 4. SHELL BORDER

In principle this border can be piped with any star-shaped decorating tube (Ateco 17, 16, 30, and 31; UK 5, 7, 14, and 27), but we are using Ateco 31 (UK 27).

Hold the piping bag at the "three o'clock" position and at an angle of approximately 45°. Set the tube on the surface of the work, and squeeze firmly. Maintain this pressure until the shell "builds up," as it were, and becomes broader. Lift the bag a little to follow the flow of icing. Now

lessen the pressure while at the same time moving your hand sharply down and to the right so that the shell ends in a point. Stop squeezing, and lift the bag away from the work. Pipe the second shell over the point of the first and to the right, building up the border shell by shell.

## 5. EDGED SHELL BORDER

This very attractive border is just right for decorating the side of a cake along the bottom edge. The border can be piped in one or two colors.

First make a shell border using Ateco tube 31 (UK 27). Remove this tube, and replace it with Ateco tube 102 (UK 11). Set the broader side under the middle of the first shell so that the narrower end of the tube is turned slightly outward. Squeeze out the icing, keeping the pressure as steady as possible, while moving your hand up and down to create a ripple. Pipe the edge in a shallow curve ending under the middle point of the next shell. The beginning of the second rippled curve overlaps the end of the first one (see the photo above). Continue in this way until the entire shell border has been edged.

## 6. SHELL AND LEAF BORDER

This is another variation of the shell

▲ To fill the piping bag: Attach the decorating tube by means of the adaptor. Turn the bag inside out to about half its length, holding the bottom end of the bag in the left hand. Spoon the stiff egg-white icing into the lower half of the bag. Hold the mass of icing in your left hand and remove the spoon. Repeat this operation until the bag is full.

The four tubes for making the decorative borders: lettering motif Ateco 4 (UK 3); star motif Ateco 17 (UK 5); petal motif Ateco 102 (UK 11); star motif Ateco 31 (UK 27).

U.K. No 3

U.K. No 5

U.K. No 11

U.K. No 27

border, and, again, you can use two colors of icing. However, the border is perhaps more distinctive when you use only one color. First pipe a border of shells using Ateco tube 31 (UK 27). Now change to Ateco 102 (UK 11). If two colored icings are being used, then you must either clean the piping bag or use another.

Hold the piping bag at the "three o'clock" position and at an angle of approximately 45°. From where the underside of each shell overlaps the next, pipe a vertical lip — this should not touch the surface of the next shell. Set the tube as deep as possible between two shells; squeeze, lift the bag away slightly, and pull it towards you. Stop squeezing, and lift the bag completely away from the work.

## 7. "UPSIDE-DOWN" SHELL BORDER

This variation of the shell border is one of the loveliest. It is particularly suitable for wedding cakes. Use Ateco tube 31 (UK 27). Begin in the same way as with the shell border — squeeze firmly, and allow the icing to build up. As the icing builds, move the bag gently towards you; then move it to the right to make a U-shaped curve. Now ease the pressure grad-

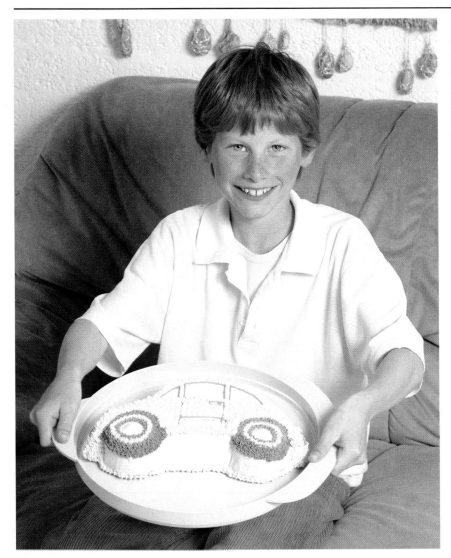

• What birthday child would not delight in receiving such a beautifully decorated "car cake"? Actually, it looks much too good to eat, but what can you do when your friends come over . . .?

You might have fun making a cake such as this with your children.

Glazed earthenware baking moulds in a wide variety of shapes — snowmen, Christmas trees, animal shapes, cars, and all sorts of other fantastic forms — can be readily obtained from specialty shops.

These are just perfect for preparing surprise cakes for children's parties. And, of course, they can be used over and over again, so that you can make a whole series of cakes all decorated in different colors! ▶

ually, and allow the icing to form a point. Make the next shell in exactly the same way, but this time the curve is "upside down" — n-shaped.

## CAKE MIXTURE FOR MOULDS

## INGREDIENTS

○ 8 oz (250 g) butter at room temperature
○ 8 oz (250 g) granulated sugar
○ a pinch of salt
○ 8 oz (250 g) plain flour or self-rising flour
○ 1 tsp. vanilla
○ 5 medium-sized eggs

*Preparation:*

Smear the inside of the baking mould with butter, and dust it with flour, tapping out any excess. Beat the rest of the butter in a mixer until it is soft, and add the sugar. Mix thoroughly, slowly adding vanilla sugar. Now beat in the eggs, one by one, only adding another when the last is well beaten into the mixture. Add a pinch of salt to the self-rising flour, and stir this into the cake mixture one spoonful at a time. Beat the mixture for several minutes until it is light and fluffy.

Fill the baking mould to three-quarters full with the mixture, and press it outward and upwards towards the sides with the back of a spoon. Bake the cake for the indicated time until it is done; it should be light brown in color. Whether the cake is done or not can be checked by piercing it with a fork: If this comes out dry, the cake is ready. Set the cake aside on a cake rack for five minutes. Turn it out.

## 8. FANTASY BORDER

This is a border that you can create yourself, making the shapes as simple or as complicated as you wish! The fantasy border is unsuitable for decorating the edges, joins, and corners of tarts and cakes, but it is, generally speaking, suitable for the sides. First pipe the basic line(s) of your pattern using Ateco tube 4 (UK 3). This basic line is a series of shallow U shapes in the photo above, rather like hanging Christmas decorations! Add the remaining elements of the pattern — different-sized dots, small circles, zigzag lines, etc.

## EQUIPMENT

### For the Volkswagen:

○ baking mould for the Volkswagen
○ 3 piping bags
○ 3 adaptors
○ Ateco tubes 17 and 31 (UK 5 and 27), small and large star motif; and Ateco 4 (UK 3), lettering motif
○ waxed paper
○ garnishing plate
○ paper towels
○ spatula

## INGREDIENTS

○ 7 oz (200 g) cake mixture (see recipe page 21)
○ egg-white icing made from two large eggs (see recipe page 11)
○ food coloring: yellow, red, and brown (mix red, green, and/or blue; a warmer tone is obtained by adding a little yellow

## EQUIPMENT

○ baking mould for the Snowman
○ 4 piping bags
○ 4 adaptors
○ Ateco tubes 17 and 31 (UK 5 and 27), star; Ateco 4 (UK 3), lettering; and Ateco 66 (UK 17), leaf motif

## INGREDIENTS

○ 8 oz (250 g) cake mixture
○ egg-white icing made from 3 eggs
○ food coloring: red, green, and brown

## Instructions — Volkswagen cake

Divide the egg-white icing into the needed portions, and add the coloring.

Cover a garnishing plate with a sheet of waxed paper, and place the cake on it. If you prefer, set both plate and cake on an icing turntable. First spread white icing for the windows, and smooth it flat with a wet knife. In the same way spread icing — with a little added color where necessary — for the wheels, the underside of the car, the headlights, the door sill, and other "smooth" parts. Pipe the contours of the windows, headlight, door handle and door using an Ateco tube 4 (UK 3).

The last stage is to fill in the large open areas with star motifs. Use Ateco 17 and 31 (UK 5 and 27) — small and large stars, respectively — in turn. You can work much more quickly with Ateco tube 31 (UK 27) but the resulting relief is rather coarser than that obtained with Ateco tube 17 (UK 5). Use the latter when you want greater detail in color and structure.

Pipe the stars close together so that no cake is visible between them. Always hold the piping bag vertically with the mouth of the tube almost touching the surface of the cake. Apply enough pressure to the bag to ensure that sufficient icing is squeezed out to form the star. Then stop squeezing, and quickly lift the tube away from the surface. Lay down the stars in vertical and horizontal bands or follow the relevant contours.

First decorate the top surface of the cake with stars and then the sides, working, as much as possible, color by color.

Finally, cut away the waxed paper, and

pipe a line of large stars with Ateco tube 31 (UK 27) along the bottom edge.

Once you have acquired a little expertise, the decorating should take between 1 and 1½ hours. Decorate the cake a few hours before you intend to cut it so that the icing remains fairly soft. If you prepare the cake the day before, then cover it with a damp cloth a few hours after decoration. This will keep the icing soft.

Instead of egg-white icing you can use the much softer water icing and butter cream. Variations in color and the detail that you are able to pipe, however, are limited to some extent by these materials.

## Instructions — Snowman cake

Also refer to the instructions for the Volkswagen cake. Cover a garnishing plate with a sheet of waxed paper, and place the cake on it. Fill piping bags with colored and plain egg-white icing. Determine the position of the eyes, nose, and mouth; pipe a drop of icing for each, and press the chocolate buttons in place. Hold the piping bag vertically with the mouth of the tube almost touching the surface of the cake. Apply just enough pressure to squeeze out sufficient icing to form the stars. Decorate the cake with the star motif, working the pattern in as you go along. Work color by

color: first the head, then the arms, and then the body. Use the Ateco 31 (UK 27) for the white icing. The brown in the head and the white in the hat are piped with the Ateco 17 (UK 5). Press in the buttons while the icing is still soft.

The decoration in the hat is piped with the Ateco 66 (UK 17) for the leaves and the Ateco 4 (UK 3) for the berries. Cut away the waxed paper, and decorate the bottom edge with a row of stars. The scarf is piped with an Ateco 17 (UK 5) held at 45°. Make a steady up-and-down movement, changing colors where indicated.

## Half rose

### EQUIPMENT

○ piping bag
○ adaptor
○ Ateco tubes 4 and 103 (UK 3 and 42)
○ waxed paper
○ garnishing plate
○ egg-white icing (see recipe page 11)
○ food coloring: red and green

Attach a piece of waxed paper to the garnishing plate with a few spots of egg-white icing, and pipe the half rose as follows.

Begin with Ateco tube 103 (UK 42). Hold the piping bag in the two o'clock position and at approximately 45°.

First make a single flat, wide petal (see page 17), and then pipe a complete rosebud in the middle of the petal. Pipe two petals over the bud, one over the left-hand side, and one over the right. Now pipe the two outer petals — these partly overlap. Hold the piping bag almost vertically, and make a turning movement with the hand. While piping the outer petals guide them upwards, towards, and against the bud. Pipe the stem in green icing using Ateco tube 4 (UK 3).

Larger or smaller budded half roses can be created by varying the number of petals.

## Narcissus or daffodil

### EQUIPMENT

○ piping bag
○ adaptor
○ Ateco tubes 61 and 2 (UK 18 and 2)
○ waxed paper
○ piece of Styrofoam
○ yellow egg-white icing
○ cornstarch

Attach a 2 × 2 in (5 × 5 cm) sheet of waxed paper to an icing nail with a spot of egg-white icing.

Using the Ateco tube 61 (UK 18) pipe six petals of the same size. Begin in the middle of the nail, and work out towards the edge; make a circular movement, and work back towards the middle, turning the nail between your fingers as you work (step 1 — see photo on page 17). The movement should be as continuous and fluid as possible, and the piping bag (and therefore the tube) should be held in a horizontal position. Repeat this procedure for all six petals (steps 2 and 3).

Dip the ends of your thumb and index finger in the cornstarch, and nip the end of the petals into a point (step 4). This must be done while the icing is still wet. Change to the Ateco tube 2 (UK 2) and pipe the cylindrical heart, layer by layer. The heart widens towards the top. When it has dried a little, pipe a zigzag edge (Ateco 2 — UK 2) along the upper rim (step 5).

## Poppy

### EQUIPMENT

○ piping bag
○ adaptor
○ Ateco tubes 102 and 2 (UK 11 and 2)
○ measuring beaker
○ aluminum foil
○ egg-white icing
○ food coloring: red and yellow

Lay a piece of aluminum foil over the mouth of a plastic cup. Push the middle in to form a hollow, and press the edges around the outside of the rim of the cup (see page 25). Take up the piping bag with Ateco tube 102 (UK 11) and red icing. The tube's wider end should be at the bottom and the narrower end up. Begin to pipe in the middle of the aluminum foil hollow.

Pipe a large, wavy petal just as described in step 1 for the daffodil. The "waves" are created by making short up-and-down movements with the piping bag. Make a circular movement from the middle to the edge, and then move back towards the center. Repeat this procedure for the next three petals (steps 2 and 3). Make sure that the petals overlap slightly.

Push up the foil a little so that the petals stand slightly more upright. Pipe a second row of petals inside the first, beginning with the first petal in the deepest part of the heart (step 4).

Finally, pipe the yellow heart using the Ateco tube 2 (UK 2). The icing can take up to two days to dry, depending on its thickness. When it is dry, remove the aluminum foil, and draw the dark lines with a non-toxic ink pen.

## CLEANING

It is important that you clean the decorating tube with a paper towel each time before you begin to pipe. This step should become automatic!

Whenever you stop work it is always possible that a last drop or two of icing squeezes out of the tube. When exposed to air, even for a minute or two, the outer surface of these drops dries a little, and this considerably reduces the adhesive quality of the icing. Keep a paper towel handy so that you can wipe the mouth of the tube clean each time before piping a new figure. By taking this precaution you prevent the icing remaining in the tube from not binding to the cake or to the icing that you have already applied.

## TECHNIQUE

Of course, it is possible that you've never done this sort of work before and that you want to try out the icing techniques just to see how they're done! In this case you can accomplish quite a lot with only one piping bag and one adaptor, provided the figures are not too complicated and you do not use too many colors.

The disadvantage is that you spend so much time cleaning the bag and the adaptor. If you do work with this technique, complete *everything* color by color to minimize how many times you have to clean your equipment.

For this type of icing work you really need at least 3 adaptors and 4 piping bags (one kept in reserve).

## CHANGING DECORATING TUBES

When you are piping flowers, quite often you will have to change the decorating tube in the middle of your work. You need two hands to do this. To free your hands while you are changing tubes, stick the icing nail into a block of Styrofoam. This material can be bought in hardware or flower shops.

Egg-white icing is not only suitable for use as a mortar for fixing candy, sugar cubes, and cake in place, but also is very useful for temporarily attaching waxed paper to a garnishing plate or an icing nail. This mortar is also known simply as "sugar paste."

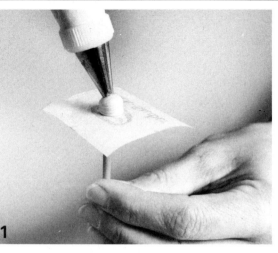

**1**

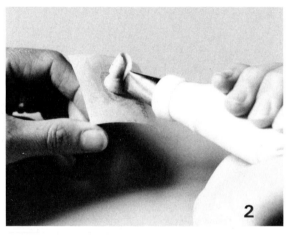

**2**

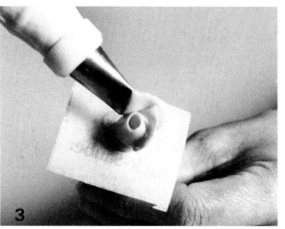

**3**

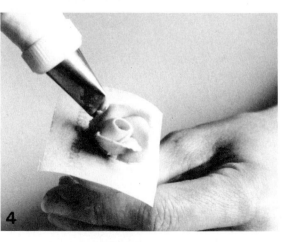

**4**

## Whole rose

### EQUIPMENT

○ piping bag
○ adaptor
○ Ateco tubes 103 and 4 (UK 42 and 3)
○ icing nail
○ waxed paper
○ piece of Styrofoam
○ egg-white icing pink/ red (see recipe page 11)

Refer to the various steps also on page 17.

Step 1: Fix a piece of waxed paper to the nail with a spot of egg-white icing. Press it down firmly. Hold the piping bag vertically, and pipe a slightly tapering "stump" of icing, using the Ateco 4 tube (UK 3) — photo 1. Hold the mouth of the tube actually in the icing. Squeeze firmly to begin with, and gradually ease the pressure.

Step 2: Change to Ateco tube 103 (UK 42). Hold the bag in approximately the two o'clock position and at 45°. Hold the mouth of the tube against the icing "stump," close to the top, with the narrow end up and slightly inward. Turn the icing nail counterclockwise while piping a strip of icing. The movement is first up, then around, and finally back down to the starting point so that a bud is formed — photo 2.

Step 3: Hold the piping bag at a right angle to the bud with the narrow end up and turned slightly outward. Begin halfway up the bud, and pipe three upright petals. Turn the nail clockwise while moving the nozzle up and down in the form of a curve — photo 3.

Step 4: Pipe the second row of four petals *below* the first row. Again turn the nail clockwise. Set the four petals such that each overlaps two of the previous petals. Turn the tube's narrow end a little more to the outside so that the petals in this row are slightly more open — photo 4.

Step 5: Pipe the last row of seven petals under those in the second row, beginning below the middle of any one of them. Direct the tube's narrow end still further to the outside so that the rose becomes even more open. When the rose is completed, remove it (together with the paper) from the icing nail, and set it aside to dry for at least twenty-four hours. If you omit step 5, you obtain beautiful roses "in bud." It is a good idea to make a few of these budded

roses to provide extra variation to the finished decoration. The green leaves are piped directly onto the cake using Ateco tube 66 (UK 17).

Note: If you wish to make larger roses (or other flowers), use the same type of decorating tube but in a larger size.

▲ This beautiful rose cake is made in three stages. First the flowers are made — at least two days earlier. The white icing layer is applied the day before the cake is finally decorated.

◀ Top left are the icing nails on which the rose and daffodil are piped. In the middle is the cup used in piping the poppy.

*Basic recipe* for an un-filled cake approximately 1¾ in (4½ cm) high. The filled cake in the photos consists of two of these cakes.

## INGREDIENTS

○ 4 oz (120 g) flour
○ 1 oz (30 g) cornstarch
○ a pinch of salt
○ 6 medium-sized eggs at room temperature
○ 6 oz (180 g) sugar
○ 1 tsp. vanilla

## STORING EGG-WHITE ICING

Egg-white icing (colored or plain) can be stored for several days in the refrigerator, provided it is sealed in an air-tight plastic container. Take the icing out of the re-frigerator several hours before you intend to use it, and allow it to slowly warm to room temperature.

If necessary, bring the existing icing to the de-sired stiffness by adding a bit more egg white, food coloring, and sieved confectioners' sugar. Egg-white icing that will be used the next day can be stored overnight sim-ply in a cool place in a closed container.

## PREPARING THE CAKE

Use a springform cake pan 10 in (26 cm) in diameter. Grease the inside with butter, and dust with flour (shaking out any excess). Put the eggs, sugar, and vanilla in a deep bowl; set the bowl in a larger bowl of hot water, and beat for approximately 20 minutes until the mixture is thick and creamy. The mixture is ready when it hangs off the beater in a "stalactite." Remove the bowl from the water.

Mix the flour, cornstarch, and salt in a sieve, and add this gradually to the mixture, folding it in well using a metal spoon. When almost all of the flour has been folded into the mixture, scrape the spoon around the bottom of the bowl to make sure that there are no flour remnants.

Add the mixture to the springform cake pan until it is two-thirds full, and set it on an oven tray in a prewarmed oven. Bake the cake following the instructions below.

Electric or gas oven: 360–390°F (180–200°C, Mark 3/4); position: bottom of the oven; baking time: 40–50 minutes.

High-performance oven: 300°F (150°C); position: bottom of the oven; baking time: 40–50 minutes.

The cake is ready when it is light brown in color and feels "springy" to the touch. Ease the cake away from the sides of the springform with a knife, and turn it out onto a baking tray. Turn it upside down, and remove the base of the springform, using a long, pointed knife if necessary.

Set it aside to cool. Immediately after the cake has cooled, it can be worked on further. If you don't want to work on the cake right away, put it back in the spring-form, and cover it with a sheet of alumi-num foil or plastic wrap.

Attach a sheet of waxed paper to a garnishing plate with spots of egg-white icing. If you are making a filled cake, as shown in the photos on the left, then lay the bottom half on a sheet of waxed paper. Spread a jam or cream filling, and place the top half over. Make sure that the filling is about half an inch (a centimeter) from the edge of the cake so that it cannot mix with the icing when this is applied later.

Make an egg-white icing from 4 eggs (see page 11). This should not be as stiff as that used for piping. The texture is right when the icing immediately flows back into an indentation made with a spoon. It is now thin enough to flow easily over the edges of the cake. Set the cake with its

**5**

**6**

**7**

**8**

plate on an icing turntable, and pour the egg-white icing on top — photo 1.

Turn the cake slowly, spreading the icing from the middle towards the edge using a spatula — photo 2. Spread the icing as uniformly as possible so that it flows evenly over the edge of the cake — photo 3 — adding more icing where necessary. Smooth the icing around the side with a spatula — photo 4. If the icing layer is occasionally too thin, take a little extra icing on the spatula, and smooth it out using a *wet* spatula. Clean the spatula as often as necessary, wetting it each time.

Any icing that flows onto the waxed paper should be scraped up and returned to the bowl immediately. Allow the icing on the cake to dry for at least 5 hours. The cake can then be worked on further.

**Finishing the cake:** Leave the cake and garnishing plate on the icing turntable. Add the whites of the two remaining eggs to the bowl together with enough sieved confectioners' sugar to make an icing which is of sufficient thickness for piping — see page 11. Color half of this egg-white icing green. Decide approximately where on the cake the roses should be positioned, and mark this with a green line piped with an Ateco tube 4 (UK 3) — photo 5. Set the roses in their approximate positions — photo 6 — and move them about until you are satisfied with the overall effect. The whole roses are towards the center; then come the budded roses, and the half roses are towards the edge (see page 25). Change to an Ateco tube 66 (UK 17), and attach the roses by piping a spot of green icing on the backs and pressing them into place — photo 7. Pipe a few green leaves under and in between the roses (how this is done and the effect it achieves can be seen in the photo on the right and in the detail photos on page 16).

Complete the decoration for the top of the cake, and then pipe a decorating border along the bottom edge with the remaining white icing. Choose one of the patterns shown on page 16 — this cake has a shell border piped with the Ateco tube 31 (UK 27) — photo 8. Finally, attach the flowers and leaves along the side of the cake using the green icing. Allow the decoration to dry for at least 8 hours, and then carefully remove the waxed paper.

If you prefer softer icing, then finish off the cake with water icing and butter cream — see page 11.

## DECORATING THE CAKE

### EQUIPMENT

- 2 piping bags
- 2 adaptors
- Ateco tubes 4, 66, and 31 (UK 3, 17, and 27)
- waxed paper
- garnishing plate
- icing turntable
- spatula
- paper towels
- already hardened whole roses, budded roses, and half roses (make sure you have a sufficient supply)
- 2 cakes 1¾ in (4½ cm) thick (see opposite page)

### INGREDIENTS

- egg-white icing made from 6 eggs (see recipe page 11)
- food coloring: green

▲ Pipe the leaves with Ateco tube 66 (UK 17). Set the mouth of the tube on the icing. Squeeze firmly, holding the mouth in the same position so that the leaf can build up in width. Then move the piping bag to one side; first very slowly, then with increasing speed so that the leaf comes to a narrow point. At that moment stop squeezing, and quickly pull the bag away from the surface. While piping make short, up and down movements to create the "waves" in the leaf.

Leaf motif Ateco 66 (UK 17)

# Candy dolls from peppermint sticks, chewing gum balls, and egg-white icing

▲ The Candy family on parade! Mom and Pop are 3½ in (8½ cm) tall (shown life-size in the photo above) and consist of a decorated piece of cinnamon stick and a chewing gum ball. The candy children are made from two large sugared almonds.

The four "Candies" seen from behind. Notice how Mom's coat is worked with a large star motif and how the hair styles of both Mom and Pop Candy are piped.▼

You will be on a firm footing when you make these little candy dolls — literally on a firm footing, as they all stand firmly on a "footing" of egg-white icing!

This is very important because without this firm base, the dolls would not stand upright.

Candy dolls are perfect for children's parties. Decorate the birthday or party cake with them, or present them as farewell gifts to the guests as they leave. Begin with the simpler examples, such as the dwarf on the right or the cinnamon and peppermint stick figures. After a little experience, you can move on to the more complex clowns (above left) or the rather stylishly dressed figures below.

These sweet, pastel-tinted little animals are more difficult to make than they appear to be at first. They are made from many more varieties of small candies than are their owners, pictured above.

Making these dolls offers good practice in piping of complex figures.

◀ For the cinnamon or peppermint figures make a shallow hack saw cut all around the stick, 2½ in (6 cm) from one end, and snap it off cleanly.

# EQUIPMENT

○ piping bag, adaptor(s)
○ Ateco tubes 2, 4, 17, 16, 66, 31, and 47 (UK 2, 3, 5, 7, 17, 27, and 34).
○ garnishing plate
○ waxed paper

# INGREDIENTS

○ cinnamon and peppermint sticks, chewing gum balls, and other candies
○ egg-white icing (see recipe page 11)
○ food coloring

Clean the hacksaw with a wire brush.

◀ The ends of the sticks must be smooth and square. This is achieved by rubbing them on a sheet of coarse sandpaper. Keep the sticks perpendicular to the sandpaper.

◀ Pipe several medium-sized stars on a sheet of waxed paper to form the footings. Press the cinnamon and peppermint sticks into them vertically.

◀ Pipe a large star (using uncolored egg-white icing) on the top of each stick, and press in a chewing gum ball to form the head of the doll. Set these basic figures aside for 24 hours to dry. Then loosen them gently from the waxed paper.

# INSTRUCTIONS

Fill the piping bag with egg-white icing (see page 11). The icing should be so stiff that a knife indentation does not disappear but remains in the icing surface. If the icing becomes thinner after awhile, add a little sieved confectioners' sugar. Attach a sheet of waxed paper to a garnishing plate with a few drops of icing. Pipe several stars on the paper with Ateco tube 16 or 31 (UK 7 or 27), (large star motifs). Cut several peppermint and cinnamon sticks to the desired lengths and set these (or chewing gum balls) exactly in the middle of the stars. Make sure they are vertical. Complete the basic figures as shown in the illustrations on this page, and set them aside for 8 hours to dry. The figures are then ready to be "dressed."

Prepare the icing to the required stiffness and color(s). The more colors you want, the more piping bags you need. The figures on the two previous pages may inspire you — but also let your imagination free! Once you have acquired the taste for making candy dolls, you will find the possibilities are endless!

The bond between the icing and candy should be as strong as possible, and therefore it is important to clean the decorating tube frequently with tissue or paper towels (see page 23). Moreover, the spots of icing mortar should not be too small, and the parts should be pressed together firmly.

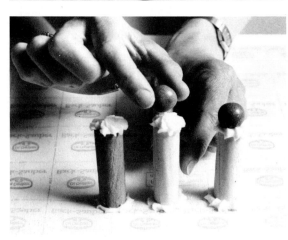

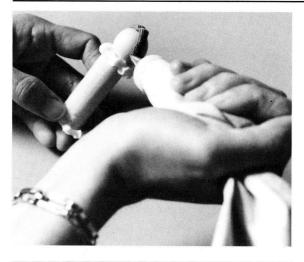

◀ Take the basic figure in one hand, and pipe with the other. While working, support both arms or elbows on a flat surface. Pipe the hair with a UK 34.

Ribbed motif UK 34

If possible work with a different piping bag for each different color. When necessary clean the tubes in lukewarm water, and dry them thoroughly. ▼

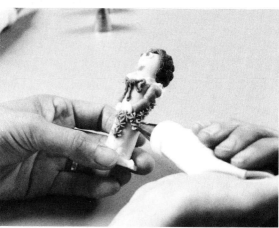

◀ The arms, nose, mouth, eyes, and bow are piped with a UK 3.

First attach the feet to the underside. Place the figure on its back, and leave for 24 hours to dry. Then attach the head and tail. Leave again for 24 hours, and then finish off.

◀ Pipe the jacket and other articles of clothing with Ateco tube 17 (UK 5), star motif.

When you are working with several colors at once, the icing just at the end of the decorating tube may begin to dry. If this occurs, clean out the mouth with a toothpick or with a pointed kitchen knife.▶

# Still more candy . . .

▲ Order out of chaos: presentation is a simple art, especially when working with licorice candies. Keep the basic idea simple — as in the straight-line pattern above. The powerfully contrasting colors create enough tension in the arrangement.

Peppermints and other ▶ black-and-white candies are even more enticing when they are set out in a simple decorative pattern.

These types of candy ▶ are too small to make hanging streamers — but just big enough to make necklaces. Candies used for stringing must be soft. Left: fruit candies (apricot, strawberry, banana, raspberry, and blueberry). Right: an assortment of candy drops.

Candy may well be bad ▶ for your teeth, but the barbecue skewers quickly disappear when children are around — and you can't say that for some things! Just don't forget that six-month visit to the dentist! ▼

Decorating trees is ▶ something that you needn't confine to Christmas — it is a marvelous idea for an outdoor children's party. Don't leave the marshmallows hanging too long — insects are also wild about these candies! Of course, decorations such as these are suited to the Christmas tree — a guaranteed success with children, young and old.

◀ This necklace is both pretty and tasty. Give each guest one as a farewell gift at the end of the children's party.

◀ A revolving cake stand or a modelling turntable (see photo) is very useful, especially when you are making circular patterns. It is not only easier and more pleasant to work in this manner but also it is quicker.

This is important when you have to incorporate lots of small candies into a pattern.

## PRESENTING CANDY ATTRACTIVELY

No matter what sort of candy you select, the illustrations on the previous pages show that you need fairly large quantities! By "large quantities" we mean quantities of about 2 to 3 lb (1 to 1½ kg). What we regard as a "normal" quantity — ¼ lb (100 g) — is used up in no time, even in the simplest of patterns!

Choose a plate or serving dish of suitable size for the quantity of candy you are working with. Use loose (unpackaged) candy as much as possible so that if you find you have less than you need, you can buy just enough extra for your needs. Alternate small and large pieces in your patterns. If you are making a mathematical or abstract figure, it is not usually necessary to draw a design first — simply begin, and it works itself out! Make sure that there is a pleasant distribution of color within the whole pattern, and fill the spaces between large pieces of candy with small pieces. Use a pair of tweezers, if necessary, to move and position each piece.

Preferably use a serving dish that has a vertical edge. Fill the dish completely so that the pattern is enclosed and the candy cannot slide about. When making rounded patterns, begin in the middle, and work your way outward in a clockwise direction. There are no hard and fast rules as to how you should approach this work, but unusually attractive results can be achieved by using a large number of shades of one particular color (plus white). Good examples of this can be seen on page 117 (the roof of the candy house) and on page 32 (the black-and-white arrangement).

If you want to arrange the candy to form a "picture" (cartoon characters from comics and television make ideal subjects, and children love them!), then it is a good idea to make a full-size drawing before you begin. You can do this with the aid of the "grid-technique". First choose your character from a comic, a magazine, or a children's book, and draw a ¼-in (5-mm) grid over it. Now draw a larger grid on a separate sheet of paper — the size of the squares depends on how large you want the finished figure to be. A ½-in (10-mm) grid will double the original size of the figure, a 1-in (20-mm) grid will quadruple the original size, and so on. Transfer the figure square by square from the original grid to the new one. Lay the drawing on a dish, and build up the figure in different colored candies, working from the middle outward. The best results are obtained by using very small pieces, very close together.

In much the same way the name and birth date of a child, an anniversary message, or Easter, Thanksgiving, and yuletide wishes can be incorporated into a candy pattern.

## EQUIPMENT

○ turntable
○ tweezers
○ toothpicks (long)
○ strong thread (e.g., for buttons)
○ large sharp-pointed needle
○ waxed paper
○ bottle of water
○ bowl of water

## INGREDIENTS

○ candies of various sorts and sizes
○ egg-white icing
○ confectioners' sugar

# FESTIVE DECORATION

To make candy chains, barbecue skewers, and tree decorations, the candy must be threaded or mounted. This means that the candy chosen must be soft — on the outside as well as the inside — so that holes can be pierced through readily. When pieces of candy are mounted in this way, they can be easily pushed out of shape, and this will cause a hard "shell" to crack or split. The hardest suitable candies are licorice candies (see page 32, left), and even these are too hard to be mounted with a needle and thread unless they are first "drilled out" with a sharp toothpick.

This is by no means an easy process, and there is a good chance that the toothpick will slip or even break. It is important that the toothpicks are thoroughly wetted before you begin to "drill," so that they slide easily through the candy. Presoak them for a few hours, and, while working, wet the points or change toothpicks at frequent intervals.

Marshmallows, lozenges, gum balls, and wine drops are all suitable for threading. Care must be taken, however, because most of these are so soft that they can easily disintegrate as they are handled. They also contain a great deal of sugar, and after a few have been threaded, you may find that so much sugar has been deposited on the needle and thread that it becomes impossible to work. In this case, simply clean them both in a bowl of warm water. Make sure that the needle and thread are dry before continuing to work — drops of water can dissolve sugar and discolor the surface.

The marshmallows for the stars are "glued" together with thick egg-white icing (see page 11). Do this on waxed paper so that the stars can be easily removed after they have dried (allow 24 hours).

The upside-down chalice-shaped hanging decorations consist of 1 large and 2 small marshmallow shapes. The latter are attached to the former with egg-white icing. These shapes must be cut out very carefully using a sharp knife (a hobby knife is ideal). The trick is to place the knife in the correct position, and then press down sharply. If you try to cut the marshmallow using the more usual "sawing" action, it will tend to stick to the knife, and the shape will be spoiled. Clean the knife frequently in water, and dry it thoroughly each time before restarting work.

◄ Before licorice candies can be threaded, you must make holes in them with a toothpick. Be careful not to damage the candies while you are doing this. Wet toothpicks are best — they cause less damage, and the candies slide over them more easily. Don't pull the stick back; push it all the way through the candies.

◄ Frequently clean the needle and thread, all the other tools, and your hands in water to dissolve the sticky sugar deposits. Dry everything thoroughly before you continue work. Of course, be careful not to splash water on the candies.

◄ The easiest way to cut spongy marshmallow is to place a sharp knife where the cut should be, and then press down in one clean, sharp movement. Very sharp scissors can also be used as shown.

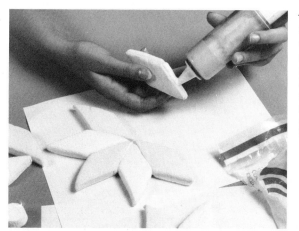

◄ A thick egg-white icing is used for fixing the candies in position. Remember that the icing requires from 18 to 24 hours to dry. Only then can the figures be removed from the waxed paper (a broad spatula is the best tool for this).

# Celebrating Easter with homemade meringue and ready-made chocolate

Children will be pleasantly surprised — and adults too — when they receive such a beautiful Easter egg. In general, a ◀ large egg already decorated such as this — base area 5 × 8 in (12 × 20 cm), height 8 in (20 cm) — is not only difficult to find in shops but also is very expensive once you do find one! But with some skill and imagination — and perhaps a bit of improvisation — you can make just such a fairy tale Easter egg for about a third or half the cost in the store, depending on what chocolate and candy bar you already have in your cupboard versus what you have to buy. The only thing you absolutely have to buy, of course, is one large, plain chocolate Easter egg! The nice thing about making this egg is that the ingredients can be bought ready-made so that, in fact, there is no real cooking to do. An excellent chance for less accomplished cooks (including some husbands who may rarely see the kitchen!) to shine because this Easter egg is fun and not at all difficult.

## INGREDIENTS

○ 1 extra-large chocolate Easter egg with a flat base
○ small Easter eggs wrapped in foil
○ large chocolate block 4 × 8 in (10 × 20 cm)
○ 3 normal-sized bars of plain chocolate
○ small bar of milk chocolate for the "ladder"
○ confectionery chickens
○ chocolate flakes (or chips)
○ green sugar confetti

Once you have mastered the art of piping meringue, you will find that this material offers almost limitless possibilities. Nevertheless there are a few points to remember:

Always mix the ingredients in the correct proportions (see page 99), and don't bake at temperatures above 260°F (125°C). Leave the oven door slightly ajar.

— Work with clean, dry, and, in particular, *grease-free* utensils; otherwise the meringue will collapse.

— Don't add too much food coloring; pastel tints are much more pleasant. Don't forget to add the flavoring extract.

— Beat the meringue mixture long and hard — it must be very stiff in texture.

— Use large decorating tubes and pipe on waxed paper.

— Practise the piping intensively. If you are not satisfied with the results, scrape up the meringue, return it to the bowl, and start again! Also see pages 39 and 99.

▲ Meringue chickens — or are they ducklings — are a festive way in which to decorate your Easter table. They also taste quite delicious any day served with morning coffee (above).

Children are always ▶ pleasantly surprised when they discover a chicken in its nest at their breakfast plate!

These figures resemble ducklings (or perhaps seals!), especially when they are made with white meringue. They are also excellent decorations for cakes baked on special occasions — New Year's Day, Thanksgiving, etc. ▼

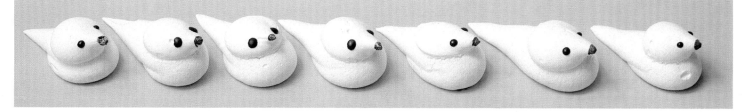

1. The ingredients (see also page 36)

2. Set a large piece of ▶ chocolate in a pan on a hot plate. When the chocolate just begins to melt (soft but not liquid) remove it from the heat. Take care if you are using an electric stove top of a gas range — these are often too hot, and the chocolate becomes too thin. Spoon a measure of thickly liquid chocolate on one corner of the chocolate block, and press the egg carefully in place. Hold it in position until the chocolate hardens.

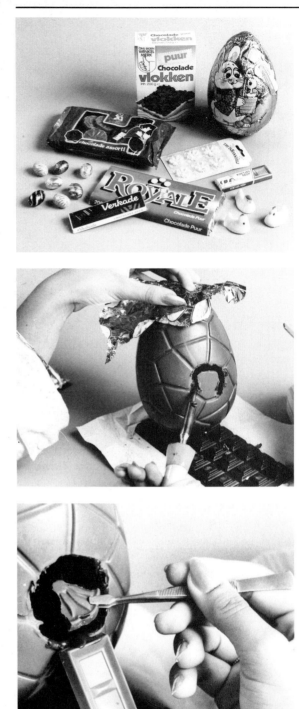

◀ 3. Cut a large hole in the side of the egg with a clean soldering iron (or a knife heated in a gas flame). Hold the egg securely at the top, using a piece of aluminum foil to keep the egg protected (and your fingers clean!).

4. Set a drop of melted ▶ chocolate on the lower lip of the hole and on the block, and press the ladder in place.

◀ 5. Break off a flat piece of chocolate to fit over the opening and the ladder. Fix it in place to form the roosting place for one lucky chicken!

6. Spread melted choc-▶ olate thickly over the base, and sprinkle chocolate flakes over it.

◀ 7. Spread melted chocolate around the entrance, using a long toothpick, and mount confectionery flowers and confetti.

8. Attach flat pieces of ▶ chocolate (in a flower motif) to the top of the egg to form the "chicken house" roof.

Note: Always be sure to allow for the time it takes the soft chocolate to cool and harden.

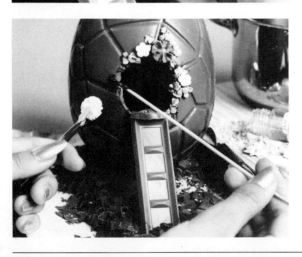

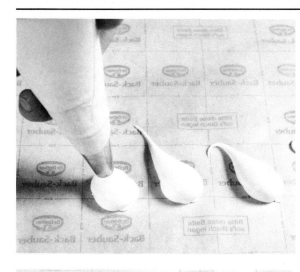

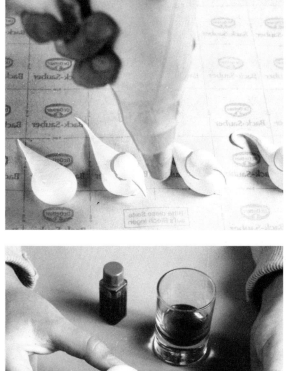

**1.** Make sufficient meringue to decorate a medium-sized tray — 2 or 3 egg whites, 4 or 6 oz (120 or 180 g) granulated sugar, respectively, a few drops of coloring, and vanilla extract. Pipe the bodies with a fairly large tube. Begin by piping a ball, then move the tube away while at the same time decreasing pressure to form the tail.

**2.** Pipe the head. Begin▶ by piping a small ball; then stop squeezing, and pull the tube sharply toward you to form the beak.

**◀3.** If the beak is too long, too thick, or the wrong shape, then adjust it to the desired form and shape with wet fingers.

**4.** After the meringue▶ has been baked, paint on the eyes with melted chocolate and the beak with red food coloring.

The size of the chickens vary from 2 to 3 in (5 to 8 cm).

**◀1.** The large mocha coffee-colored (and tasting!) nest (page 37) is 6 in (15 cm) in diameter. First pipe a base of thick meringue — 5 in (13 cm) diameter — in green, yellow, or dark brown.

**2.** Using a smaller noz-▶ zle and with a short twisting movement, pipe a crisscross pattern with mocha meringue.

**◀3.** Sprinkle shaved almonds over the "nest" immediately; then put it in the oven to bake.

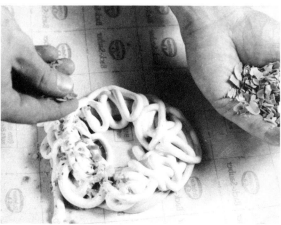

**1.** For a private little▶ nest 3 in (8 cm) in diameter, first pipe a closed spiral for the base and then build up the wall layer by layer.

# Bread in its Easter finery . . .

Easter men: 6 × 4 in (16 × 12 cm); large chicken below: 7 × 7 in (18 × 18 cm); Easter hare: 5 × 10 in (13 × 26 cm); cockerel: 9 × 11 in (22 × 28 cm); flower: 7 × 14 in (18 × 36 cm). These rough dimensions are for unbaked dough.

▲ What fun and how easy it is to give your little bread men an egg to hold for Easter! Place an uncooked egg between the arms before you put the figure in the oven. The egg will cook along with the bread.

Pastry modelling al-▶ lows you to use your imagination creatively. All sorts of shapes and patterns can be made. Remember, however, that this type of bread won't stay fresh for very long.

It's not only a pleasant idea, but a very tasty one: homemade bread — hot from the oven — as the centerpiece of the family table on Easter Sunday. Why not encourage the whole family to join in the bread-making on Easter morning? After all, they say many hands make light work (bread?). Take into account the size of your oven — especially if you have a large family with healthy appetites!

If you have never baked bread before, it might be a good idea to get in a little practice beforehand. The weekend before Easter provides an excellent opportunity — the children can invite their friends around

◄ The dough is rolled in 3 phases (see text). Fold the ends over to form two loops.

◄◄ Take the end of the pastry loop, and fold it underneath and back up through the loop to form a thumb knot. You can make various designs with similar lengths of dough: 18 in (45 cm).

## INGREDIENTS

○ 2 lb (1000 g) flour
○ 1½ oz (40 g) fresh yeast (obtainable at a bakery) or ¾ oz (20 g) dried yeast.
○ ¾ oz (20 g) salt
○ ⅜ oz (10 g) light brown sugar
○ 1½ oz (40 g) butter
○ 17 fl oz (5 dl) water
○ 1½ oz (½ dl) milk
○ uncooked eggs (as required)

*Egg glaze recipe*: 2 yolks mixed with 1 white.

When you are making the bread figures, brush all connecting surfaces with egg glaze to promote a good bond between the parts.

◄ After the dough has risen, roll it out into a sheet ⅜ to ⅝ in (1 to 1½ cm) thick. Cut out all the parts of the flower. Work on a plain wooden surface sprinkled with flour.

Smear a baking tray with butter. Position the stem, petals, heart, and leaves. Where two parts overlap, brush egg glaze on the dough to achieve a good bond. Press the parts firmly together; be careful not to distort or damage them in any way.

◄ Press lines in relief as desired using a plastic spatula, the back of a knife, or a cookie cutter. Brush the entire figure once or twice with egg glaze (let dry before applying the second coat). This ensures that the figure will be a lovely golden brown.

on Palm Sunday to sample the (successful) results of your hard work!

Of course, baking your own bread need not be confined to Easter. There are plenty of other festive occasions throughout the year — and fresh home-baked bread is a tasty treat at any time. Baking is also an excellent way for the children to have fun on a rainy day at home — success is guaranteed!

Begin with a number of simple figures such as Easter men or "plaited" bread (top left and above).

There are two methods of going about baking your own bread — you can buy a packet of ready-made bread mix (in which case follow the instructions on the packet), or you can make your own dough from the ingredients given here. All the shapes illustrated here were prepared from these ingredients and according the instructions given below.

## INSTRUCTIONS

Add the milk to the water, and bring this to a temperature of 95°F (35°C). Dissolve the yeast in the mixture, and add the whole to the flour. Mix into a firm mass. Add the salt, sugar, and butter, and kneed firmly for 10 to 25 minutes until the dough is supple and elastic.

Set the dough aside under a damp cloth for 15 minutes to allow it to rise. Bubbles of air form during this process, and these must be removed by repeatedly pressing the dough flat or beating it against a firm surface.

You can now begin to model the figures. Work as quickly as possible, since the dough continues to rise, and it must be put in the oven within three-quarters of an hour. The lengths of dough (for plaited bread, arms, and legs) are rolled in three stages with two minute pauses in between, the length becoming longer at each stage. Do not sprinkle flour on the working surface, and roll out the dough with the

The Easter cockerel is ▶ built from several parts (thickness — ⅜ to ⅝ in (1 to 1½ cm). This figure just fits a normal-sized baking tray. Any sharp pastry edges are rounded off with a wet finger.

◀ Smear the baking tray with butter. For the head make a little ball of dough, and flatten it slightly. The bottom of the ball, which is the neck, must be a little flatter than the head.

◀ Roll out a 16 in (40 cm) length of dough, approximately ¾ in (2 cm) thick, in 3 phases. Position it against the neck to form the body and legs. Brush egg glaze where this joins the neck to ensure a good bond. Set the egg in place just below the hollow of the neck.

◀ Roll a shorter, some-what thinner, length for the arms. Place them around the egg.

When the modeling is ▶ complete, brush at least one coat of egg glaze over the figure so that, after baking, the surface is a lovely golden brown.

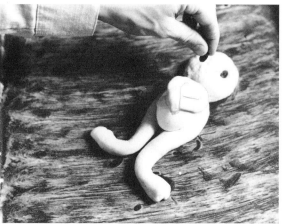

◀ Push the currant eyes ¼ in (½ cm) deep into the dough so that they remain in position and won't fall out during baking. Brush the whole figure with egg glaze. Let it rise further, and bake it for 10 to 15 minutes. Immediately after baking, brush the surface with water to give a lovely surface gloss. Set the figures aside on a baking rack to cool.

palms of both hands. This method of preparation prevents the bread from breaking up at a later stage. Keep the bread figures more or less flat — the dough should not be thicker than about ½ to ¾ in (1 to 1½ cm) — to minimize the chance of surface cracks appearing. Read the captions to the photos on these pages for all the further instructions you may require. When you have completed the figures, brush the surface with beaten egg yolk, and leave

them for a half hour to rise further. If they dry out during this period, spray them lightly with water (using a plant sprayer) or brush more egg yolk onto the surface.

In the meantime preheat the oven to 390–400°F (200–225°C) or Mark 5/6, and bake the bread for 10 to 15 minutes. The bread is ready as soon as it emits a hollow sound when you tap it firmly. Immediately after the bread is removed from the oven, the surface should be brushed with water in order to obtain a beautiful glaze. Set the bread aside on a baking tray to cool.

# Fantasy bread, rolls, and buns

◀ Here is a festive idea for a simple cold lunch, especially if you have something to celebrate! One glimpse of this Fun Food is enough to stir the appetite of most children — no matter how absorbed they might be in what they are doing!

The best way to serve these sandwiches is on a tray, but separately can be a lot of fun, too. But always be careful to warn children and adults alike of the many toothpicks holding the delightful faces and garnishings in place. Perhaps the toothpicks should be removed before you let the children begin devouring.

Bread and buns must not only look good, they must also taste good; it is therefore very important that they are absolutely fresh. It is best to buy fresh rolls from the baker rather than the supermarket — you never know how long they've been sitting inside the plastic wrapping! Preparation goes more quickly (and is more fun) when there are two. In this way one can, for example, butter the rolls while the other positions the decorations. Before you begin, prepare all necessary ingredients, and set them out separately on platters or in bowls.

Bread is available in a wide variety of rolls and buns at the bakery — white or brown, round or torpedo-shaped, hard or soft, with or without sesame or poppy seeds. In short, choice enough for any taste! ▼

The quickest way to prepare sandwich rolls is merely to stuff in one or another filling! Making these Fun Food rolls, however, takes a little more thought and effort because, in order to achieve the maximum visual effect, all of the fillings and garnishings must be positioned carefully, more or less precisely.

The photos on this page are intended to inspire your imagination: once you start to work, you will find that you soon begin to invent variations of your own.

## EQUIPMENT

○ sharp serrated bread knife
○ toothpicks
○ various dishes and bowls
○ flat aluminum trays to set out the rolls for serving

## INGREDIENTS

○ various rolls (round and oblong)
○ butter
○ cold cuts (ham, salami, etc.)
○ slices of cheese
○ firm tomatoes
○ cucumber
○ lettuce leaves
○ garden cress
○ parsley
○ cocktail onions
○ pickled onions
○ gherkin pickles
○ blueberries
○ radishes
○ hard-boiled eggs
○ stuffed olives

Cut a soft poppy seed roll open just below the middle, and spread butter on both halves. Lay a lettuce leaf on the bottom half so that it protrudes on all sides. Take a square slice of cheese, and lay it diagonally over the lettuce leaf. Roll a "tongue" from a slice of ham; lay it on the cheese, and close the roll. Make the eyes from two radishes, and fix them in place with toothpicks. The toothpicks should pass right through the roll, and hold the other ingredients — including the ham tongue — in place. For the ears fix two slices of tomato also with toothpicks.

Cut a brown sesame seed bun open just below the middle, and spread butter on both halves. Lay slices of egg and tomato so that the last large slice of tomato protrudes from the roll to form the "lips" or a "tongue." Lay parsley or garden cress so that it sticks out of the sides and back to form the "hair." Toothpicks fix in position two pickled onions for the eyes and two blueberries for the nose. The toothpicks also hold the other ingredients in place.

Cut a long bread roll open just below the middle, and spread both halves with butter. Lay a lettuce leaf together with a few slices of egg on the bottom half. Position two medium-thick slices of tomato at one end so that they protrude a little. Fix two blueberry "eyes" in position with toothpicks. These also hold the slices of tomato in place. Cut a shallow groove along the middle of the top of the roll, and carefully insert three thin half-slices of cucumber — the grooves must not be too deep, otherwise the roll will fall apart.

Cut a bun open just below the middle, and spread both halves with butter. Lay slices of cucumber so that they protrude slightly from the sides. Lay a square slice of ham on top of the cucumber. The lips are made with a slice of tomato and a slice of cucumber. Close the roll and push two toothpicks through to hold all the ingredients in place. Set two blueberries on the points of these toothpicks for the eyes, and use a third stick to position the radish nose. The cucumber eyebrows are set round the blueberries.

# Looks good enough to frame . . .

Anything you can do with bread rolls you can also do with ordinary slices of bread or large rusks. The possibilities are limitless — from simple patterns to beautiful "pictures" that look good enough to frame! And the preparation is not nearly so difficult as you may think — the secret is in setting the ingredients out before you begin. With the examples on these pages as your starting point — and with a little imagination — you will very soon be "composing" your own "pictures."

This method of decorating bread is also less "fussy" than decorating bread rolls because you do not need toothpicks to fix the ingredients together.

What you do need, however, is a sufficient variety of ingredients (see page 51). The quantity, of course, depends on the number of slices you intend to prepare. Moreover, some ingredients (carrots, parsley, chives, peppers, etc.) — although essential — are only needed in small quantities. In this case it may be more economic to buy packs of soup vegetables rather than separate ingredients by the bunch or by weight. In any case, roughly work out what you will need before you visit the supermarket. One further point: make sure that all of your ingredients are as fresh as possible!

Before you begin, clean your working surface thoroughly, and set out all the ingredients separately on platters or in bowls. This is absolutely essential — it is quicker and much more pleasant to work when you have a good overall view of your "color palette" of vegetables, herbs, sliced meats and cheeses, and garnishings. Place the herbs — parsley, chives, celery, etc. — in separate glasses of water to keep them fresh. Clean the radishes — remove the heads but not the roots — and set them in a bowl of water. Do the same with the baby carrots. Keep sliced meats and cheeses in the refrigerator until you need them.

Butter the bread right before you begin to decorate it, as slices of bread stay fresh for a much shorter time than do rolls. When you are preparing a large number of slices (for guests or a children's party), it is

Slices of cheese and ▶ fine-textured cold cuts can be cut directly with a cookie cutter. If this proves difficult, then cut around the shape with a sharp-pointed knife. Take care to cut a good, clean shape — cold cuts sometimes have tiny bits of fat or gristle which can be awkward to cut cleanly.

Line detail — such as ▶ door and window frames, wheel spokes, and flower stems — are made with chives. Cut the chives to the required length, and position them using a pair of tweezers.

Trees and bushes are ▶ made with a hollow stem of chive into which a small head (or heads) of parsley is mounted.

When sprinkling chips ▶ ensure that there is enough butter on the bread to hold them in place. Don't use too much, however, or the clear contours of the shapes will be lost.

The best results are obtained using a cookie cutter. Before removing it from the surface of the bread, press the chips firmly in place with your finger. This is particularly important with small details such as arms and legs.

◄ Butter — a lettuce leaf — 2 thin strips of cucumber (with skin) — a few leaves of celery — 2 radish "flowers" (see page 61), cut in half, and a spot of tomato ketchup in the heart of the "flowers."

Butter — a square slice ▶ of ham — a round slice of cheese — cress — 2 half slices of cucumber with halves of radish on top — a triangular piece of salami — tomato ketchup, and mayonnaise.

◄ Butter — 2 lengths of chives — salami — thin slices of radish, and mayonnaise "clouds."

Butter — square slice ▶ of cheese — sprig of celery with two leaves — thin slices of radish — one halved-radish flower (see page 61).

Butter — 6 thin slices of cucumber — a hard-boiled egg cut lengthwise — a slice of a hard-boiled egg — 2 slivers of cucumber and 1 of tomato (with skin) for the eyes and mouth — 4 halved gherkins — ◄ tomato ketchup.

Butter — a slice of ▶ luncheon meat — chives — 2 large rectangular flat pieces of cucumber — a thin strip of cucumber (with skin) — a small square flat of cucumber (with skin) — two halved lengths of carrot — two half slices of radish (as thick as the cucumber that is positioned under and supports the half-radish "wheels").

The larger the slice of ▶ bread, the lovelier the "picture"! If you find the fillings a little thin in places, then spread a layer of cream cheese over the butter before placing the other elements. Ingredients: chives, radish, garden cress (sprinkled over the mayonnaise), parsley, cucumber, cheese, smoked pork sausage, luncheon meat, mayonnaise, and tomato ketchup.

A thinly sliced French ▲ loaf can be transformed into an alligator by attaching two radish eyes with toothpicks and piping two nostrils with mayonnaise. Slice the jaws at a slight angle, and force them carefully apart. Set a lettuce leaf in the mouth together with a radish to keep it open.

Rusks can be decorated just as slices of bread, even though they are on the small side! When using sprinkled decorations make sure you have ◀ a good color contrast.

best to make several "prints" of one pattern before starting a new one.

If you have help, set up a production line: one to butter, one to lay slices or meat or cheese, one to pipe garnishings, etc. This method speeds up the work enormously. Another advantage of having help is that it gives you more time to experiment, and allows you to produce a wider variety of these culinary "masterpieces"! One final tip: when you are making a design, bear in mind who is going to eat it — children, colleagues, ladies from the bridge club, etc., and for what (if any) celebration it is intended (wedding, Thanksgiving, birthday party, etc.).

**General tips:** — Use a very sharp kitchen knife to slice the ingredients.

— Keep your equipment (cutters, tweezers, etc.) and paper towels handy.

— When slices of cucumber, radish, tomato, etc. must overlap, make sure that they are cut extra thin; they adhere better to one another and do not protrude too much.

— When using "sprinkled" materials, such as chocolate sprinkles, spread a little extra butter to ensure the sprinkles "stick" to the surface. Be sparing in your use of such materials as they tend to blur the outlines. Be careful when using powdered ingredients as these tend to absorb the oil from the butter, and this can form lumps or cause discoloration.

## EQUIPMENT

- very sharp kitchen knife and bread knife
- butter knife
- tweezers
- paper towels
- cutting board(s)
- bowls or dishes
- teaspoon for sprinkling chips, etc.
- cookie cutters

## INGREDIENTS

Depending on what you wish to prepare:

- slices of cheese and cold cuts (ham, smoked pork sausage, luncheon meat, etc.)
- cucumber
- tomato
- radish
- garden cress
- parsley
- gherkin pickles
- cocktail onions
- onion
- baby carrots
- plain chocolate chips or sprinkles
- colored fruit chips
- aniseed chips
- aniseed comfits
- peanut butter
- butter
- slices of bread

Butter — small, square ▶ pieces of cheese and ham, all exactly the same size — slices of gherkin placed on the ham, radish caps on the cheese.

◀ Butter — chopped garden cress — onion rings of different diameters.

Butter — square slice ▶ of cheese — a small oval slice of cucumber (head) — parsley (hair) — 2 slivers of cucumber with skin (eyes) — a sliver of tomato with skin (mouth) — half a large slice of cucumber (body) — thin slices of radish (skirt) — tomato segments (arms).

Butter — 6 thin slices ▶ of cucumber — a round slice of cheese (face) — two small slices of the end part of a cucumber (eyes) — a diagonally cut cap from an oval radish (nose) — tomato segment with skin (mouth).

Butter — rectangular ▶ slice of cheese — a heart-shaped piece of salami or smoked pork sausage, cut using a cookie cutter, with a hole through the middle for the chives "arrow" — 1 celery leaf arrow "point" — a halved radish flower with a spot of tomato ketchup as its heart.

◀ Butter — a lettuce leaf — 2 large onion rings — half radishes without caps (eyes) — long piece of tomato with skin (mouth) — 2 spots of mayonnaise (nose).

Butter (spread thickly ▶ right to the edges of the bread) — outside a heart-shaped cookie cutter sprinkle plain chocolate chips or sprinkles, inside aniseed comfits or fruit chips. Before you remove the cutter from the surface of the bread, press the chips down gently into place. Do not sprinkle the pieces in thick layers, or it will not adhere to the butter properly.

Butter in a thin layer ▶ — thin layer of peanut butter over the whole slice — set the cookie cutter shape on the bread and sprinkle a thin layer of plain chocolate sprinkles inside.

Butter (thick layer ▶ spread to the edges) — set the cookie cutter on the bread, and sprinkle chocolate sprinkles on the outside and white aniseed comfits on the inside. Press gently into place, and remove the cutter from the bread.

## TIP

Decorated slices of bread or rusks are especially suitable for birthdays, for serving in bed on Mother's Day or Father's Day, or for cheering up someone who is not feeling well.

When the children are clamoring for an in-between-meals snack, it is not always the best thing to just shut them up with candy or fast food. Snacks of fruit and vegetables are not only better for the teeth, they are also healthier and help to relieve thirst! This is the message that the wise old cucumber men are passing on to the youngster in the photo on the left. Whether he is convinced or not is another matter! But one thing is certain: the more attractive you make these snacks, the better they will go down (literally) with the children!

All the wheels of the cucumber train are held in place with toothpicks. The heads of the mice sit in hollows cut into the cucumber with a half-round scoop. ▶

# Fresh, healthy snacks for young and old

It looks very easy — and it actually is! It is simply a matter of cutting and slicing — straight or diagonally; crosswise or lengthwise; partly or completely. If you simply experiment with the slices and chunks of ingredients, making various patterns and fixing the pieces in different ways, you will find that the figures almost create themselves!

▲ If the radish is not meant to be eaten, cloves can be used for the eyes instead of chocolate sprinkles.

▲ Standing, half-sitting, lying, or even swimming, cucumber animals can be made in almost every position and posture. Remember to take out the toothpicks before you eat the snacks — and, even more important, don't forget to warn the children to do the same!

## EQUIPMENT

- toothpicks with sharp points at both ends
- sharp, serrated, large kitchen knife
- tweezers
- wooden cutting board

## INGREDIENTS

- a number of good, straight cucumbers (how many depends on how many you intend to feed)
- large, round radishes
- plain chocolate sprinkles

## INSTRUCTIONS

Read the instructions given with each of the working photos on these pages. Prepare the basic shapes of the cucumber figures a few hours at most before serving. Do not prick out the holes for the eyes and insert the chocolate chips until just before serving — the chocolate absorbs moisture and liquifies. You can, however, mount the heads (with ears) on the cucumber bodies. After garnishing the figures, spray them with a little water to keep them as fresh as possible. Store the figures in the refrigerator.

When making the cucumber train (see pages 52 and 53, bottom photo), use a whole cucumber. Choose one that is as straight and long as possible. To make the standing or "crawling" figures (see pages 52 and 53, top photos), use only the last 4 to 6 in (10 to 15 cm) of the cucumber. In this case, choose a small cucumber to minimize waste. Actually, the middle portion can be sliced thickly and garnished as shown on page 60.

The general rule for preparing these tasty (and healthy) snacks is the same as the rule for preparing rolls and bread slices — organize all your ingredients beforehand!

To make the body, cut off the ends of cucumbers at various angles. The cut must be flat so the cucumber stands upright.

Push a toothpick into ▲ the cucumber, and mount the radish head in such a way that the base of the root forms the nose.

◀ The ears are made of thin slices of radish. Cut shallow grooves in the sides of the head, and insert the sliced radishes carefully in position.

Now position the ears ▶ and eyes. First use a toothpick to prick a hole on each side of the nose. Insert plain chocolate sprinkles into these holes with a pair of tweezers (plain chocolate gives a better color contrast). This should be done only just before serving, because the chocolate tends to absorb moisture from the radish.

## EQUIPMENT

To make these tomato flies you need:

- toothpicks pointed at both ends
- sharp serrated knife
- wooden cutting board
- various dishes or bowls
- piping bag or plastic squeeze bottle.

## INGREDIENTS

- medium-sized, firm tomato
- cucumber and/or winter radish
- small gherkin pickles
- cloves
- mayonnaise

4. Insert a toothpick into the tomato at a slight angle, and mount the head on it. The angle is necessary because the eyes should point slightly upwards (this gives the flies an air of inquisitive friendliness). When the eyes point downwards, the flies seem to be rather sad and downcast — and that is certainly not your intention! ▼▼

3. For the head use a large cocktail onion. The base of the root becomes the nose. Prick holes diagonally above the nose on each side, and insert cloves for the eyes.▼

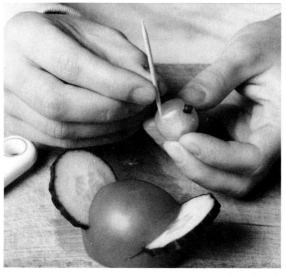

▲ 1. Cut off the bottom quarter of the tomato, and lay the larger portion on your working surface. Cut a fairly deep groove on each side of the tomato at an angle of 45°.

2. Cut thin slices of the cucumber (or winter radish), and push them carefully into these grooves. They are the fly's wings. ▶

This little family of ▶
tomato flies (the male
has large white wings
and the female smaller
green ones — *vive la
différence!*) is primarily
intended to decorate a
serving dish with stuffed
tomatoes and cucumber
snacks.

Of course, you may wish
to make the whole dish
with such flies, but this
is time-consuming work
— even though the dish
is bound to be received
with surprise and delight
by your guests. One fur-
ther suggestion: any re-
maining roots on the
cocktail onions should
be left in place as they
make good antennae (or
even mustaches!) and
not cut off.

5. For the tail take a ▶
small gherkin, and cut it
in half lengthwise. Insert
a toothpick at an angle
in the back of the
tomato, slightly below
the middle, then mount
the gherkin. If you feel
that this is one too many
toothpicks, or if you do
not like gherkins, then
pipe a mayonnaise tail in
its place.

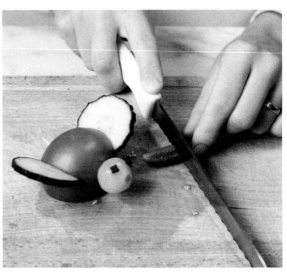

6. Pipe thin strips and ▶
tiny dots of mayonnaise
on the tomato body
using a squeeze bottle or
a piping bag (see page
59, bottom left). Clean
the opening of the
squeeze bottle at regular
intervals.

Egg-toadstools can be ▶ prepared quite quickly from hard-boiled eggs and fairly small, firm tomatoes (see page 59). The egg-bugs will surprise your guests even more, but they do require a little more work. Moreover, you need more ingredients.

Both the toadstools and the bugs are perfectly suited for making and serving in quantity. They are intended as filling snacks for adults at a cocktail party or as garnishing for a cold buffet — in which case you don't need quite so many. Serve these "egg-citing" snacks on fresh lettuce leaves or on dark green leaves of Savoy cabbage.

▲ Here is a stippled variety of bug for those who like tomato ketchup and also an attractive color contrast. In both cases apply the dots using a plastic squeeze bottle or a piping bag (see page 59).

The children might be ▶ happier if presented with egg-figures such as "Bert" and "Ernie." A little imagination and improvisation go a long way in devising figures such as these.
Don't forget to warn your family or guests that there is a toothpick in the egg!

## EQUIPMENT

For the egg-bugs:

○ kitchen knife
○ sharp serrated knife
○ wooden cutting board
○ 2 teaspoons
○ plastic squeeze bottle

## INGREDIENTS

○ cucumber
○ hard-boiled eggs
○ firm tomato
○ parsley
○ caviar or finely ground
　dried spices
○ mayonnaise

▲ 1. Cut the cucumber diagonally into oval slices approximately ⅜ in (1 cm) thick. Make sure that the cuts are parallel so that the slices are of equal and uniform thickness. Slice the hard-boiled eggs in half lengthwise.

2. Cut a tomato in ▶ slices. Cut the cap into three and use the middle triangular piece for the bugs tongue (see photo). Place it between the cucumber and egg half. Cut a thin length of tomato (with skin), and lay it along the bug's back.

3. Fill a plastic squeeze ▼ bottle with mayonnaise (see photo right), and pipe two spots for the eyes.

4. Take a few grains of ▶ caviar or a small amount of finely ground dried spices on the point of a teaspoon, and set these over the dots of mayonnaise with the tip of another spoon as shown.

## INGREDIENTS

For "Bert" (below left) and "Ernie" (right):

- hard-boiled eggs
- firm tomato
- cucumber
- parsley
- caviar or finely ground dried spices
- stuffed olives or tomato ketchup

Use a self-made piping bag of waxed paper for piping the mayonnaise or — and this is perhaps easier — a plastic squeeze bottle. You can fill this using a cream syringe. The base of the syringe should not be placed tightly in the mouth of the bottle, but held against it at a slight angle. When the mouth is sealed tight, the air cannot be displaced to allow the mayonnaise to flow freely out of the syringe. Use mayonnaise from the refrigerator as this is usually thicker. You can keep a jar of mayonnaise, which is more economical. ▼

## WORKING METHOD

Similar egg figures to "Bert" and "Ernie" can be created with a little imagination.

Cut a thin slice from one end of the egg so that the figure stands upright.

The mouth can be made in two ways: in the form of a thin strip of tomato flesh with skin that is pushed into a cut in the egg (see "Bert" in the photo, left); or in the form of a thick slice of tomato that is placed between two separate egg halves (see "Ernie" photo, right). Push a toothpick through the middle of the egg, tomato, and/or cucumber.

Mount the half-olive eyes on half toothpicks, and stick these in the egg (see "Bert" photo, left). These eyes can also be made with a thin slice of stuffed olive (see "Ernie" photo, right). The advantage is that thin slices of olive can be fixed in position just with spots of mayonnaise — they don't need toothpicks. If the children don't like olives, you can use two small half radishes, or simply pipe the eyes with tomato ketchup. Make the noses in the way as described for the egg-bugs.

For the hair, cut short lengths off the tops of parsley. Prick holes ³⁄₈ in (1 cm) deep into the top of the egg, and push in the parsley stems. Pipe Ernie's teeth in mayonnaise on the skin of the tomato mouth.

Prepare these snacks immediately before you intend to serve them. Be careful to refrigerate those figures already completed for the brief time that you are still preparing others.

A toothpick acts as ▲ the spine. If you find it necessary to handle the snacks as you serve them to your guests, then pick them up by the lowest part. For children, it is easier if you serve the egg-figures simply in a shallow dish.

Although it is not ▲ strictly necessary, you can fasten the top and bottom parts of the toadstools together with toothpicks. Add the mayonnaise dots immediately before you serve the dish.

You can quickly create these dangerous-looking snakelike creatures from two good-sized gherkins, four cocktail onions, and a sliver of red pepper, for each. With the pickled gherkins, the creatures taste as "sour" as they look!

You will achieve the most realistic effect with slightly curved gherkins. Cut off the bottom, from the back to about the middle, at an angle so that the head protrudes upwards — as if it were rising from the grass.

◀ Radish toadstools are a filling, crunchy snack to eat with a cocktail. Only the large oval varieties of radish are suitable, however.

After you have cut the radishes to shape (see page 62), place them in a bowl of cold water until just before you serve them. If you don't do this, they will soon dry out and lose both their flavor and their crunchy quality.

Present the radish toadstools on a bed of parsley or garden cress. The toadstools not only can be served as individual snacks, but they are also ideal for working into a salad landscape such as that described on page 124 or as an element of the *landed estates* in the cold buffet illustrated on page 65.

Decorative contrasting ▶ shapes made of slices of cucumber, winter radish, carrot, and yellow, red, and green peppers can be made with a variety of small cookie cutters. This is similar work to that described on page 81 for cakes.

The method is simple: the heart of one slice is set into the outline of the other, and vice versa! Note that there is sometimes a difference in thickness between the heart and the outline; this is deliberate. This variation is intended to give an extra dimension to the shapes. The slices must not be thicker than the depth of the cutters, of course.

Radishes provide a perfect opportunity to the true fruit and vegetable artist! The advantage is that the radish is fresh and firm. With a razor-sharp knife and a little patience, you can transform a simple radish into a complete sculpture, a sculpture that can be as complex as you wish to make it.

The simplest way of working with radishes is to use the special cutting tool (see page 63, top right) which cuts the radish into eight parts and leaves a cylinder-shaped heart in the middle. This tool can be bought in any store specializing in kitchen accessories. If you put the radish in cold water for a while, it opens up to form a lovely "flower" (see photo, right).

All the shapes described here open out when soaked in cold water. For the instructions see page 63.

◀ Use only firm, large oval-shaped radishes to make the toadstools. Cut off the leaves and root with a very sharp knife, taking great care not to damage the rest of the red radish skin. Cut the root off very close to its base so that as little white flesh as possible is exposed.

▲ For this type of work you need very small, sharp cookie-cutting shapes. Sets of these can be bought in most good department stores and shops that specialize in kitchen accessories. (See page 9.)

◀ Place the radish on a wooden cutting board with the root end down and the leaf end up. Place a small diameter apple corer vertically over the middle of the radish, and press it down firmly to just a little more than halfway down the radish body.

◀ Make a cut in the radish above the halfway point so that the knife comes to rest on the apple corer. Now slowly turn the corer in a full circle, while holding the knife steady, so that the cut goes all the way around the radish to where you began.

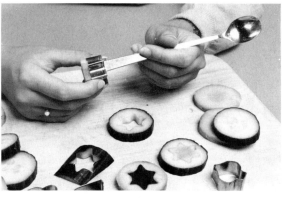

▲▲ Cut not-too-wide slices of an even thickness. They do not necessarily need to be circular — ellipses and ovals which are sliced diagonally are just as suitable. Cucumber, winter radish, or carrot can even be sliced lengthwise, although this uses up a lot more of the vegetable. Place the cutter in the middle of the slice (or at the point where the slice has good color and a smooth texture). Press firmly down with the thumbs or the palm of the hand.

▲ Twist the cutter to ensure that it has cut right through the flesh, and remove it very carefully, holding down the outside of the slice as you do so. Now push out the cut shape from the cutter using the back of a spoon or the end of a pencil.

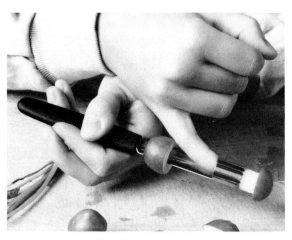

◀ Push the lower (larger) part of the radish downwards, and remove the stalk of the toadstool from the corer. If necessary cut the bottom off at right angles so that the toadstool stands upright.

Immediately after they have been cut, place the toadstools in a bowl of cold water.

Radish flowers are made with this special tool. The radish is mounted vertically on a metal tip, and the upper part of the tool is pressed down firmly. The tool has a spring action that opens easily so the cut radish can be removed. Place the radish in a bowl of cold water, and after a while it will open up. Preferably use firm, unmarked, large round radishes. First remove the leaves and root, being careful not to damage the skin. (The triangular point at the front of the cutting tool is intended for serrating halves of oranges.) ▶

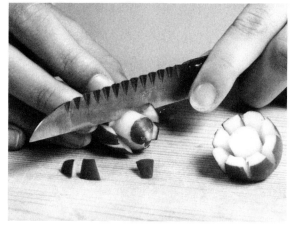

◀ The external appearance of the radish flowers that have been made with the cutter shown above can be changed by cutting away the petals and heart just above the halfway point. A second variation is to cut away only the petals, and keep the heart in its original condition.

◀ For these reliefs the radishes must be in optimum condition — they should have a sound, hard skin; there should be no sign of withering or decay; and they should be large in format. Use a very sharp knife — a utility knife is perfect. First cut the grooves lengthwise, and then cut the circular grooves — to about ⅛ in (2 mm). Let the radish soak in cold water to enhance the attractiveness of the reliefs.

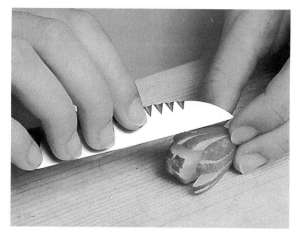

◀ Take a large, oval-shaped radish, and set it in an upright position. Slice it from the top almost to the bottom in parallel cuts about ⅛ in (2 mm) apart. Turn the radish on its side, and repeat this procedure, making cuts at right angles to the first. Leave it in cold water for a while, and it will open up to form a beautiful sea anemone.

Radish flowers can also be made with an ordinary, sharp kitchen knife. A star-shaped flower can be formed by slicing from the top almost to the bottom to make four cuts. Make sure that the eight parts are roughly the same size. The star will open up when soaked in cold water. Small changes in shape are possible by cutting off the tips of the petals or simply by cutting the radish in half crosswise. ▼

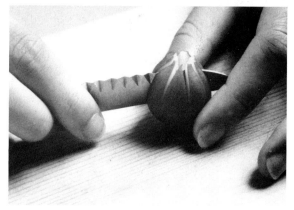

Radish roses can be made by making very very thin cuts parallel to the skin. Do this over the length (or, if you prefer, the height) in two or three layers, each layer overlapping the previous one. The number of layers you are able to cut will depend on the size and shape of the radish. As long as they have been cut deeply enough, the thin scale-like petals will open up to form a lovely rose when the radish is soaked in cold water. ▼▼

# Appetizers — architecture in classic and country style

Of course, such a deliciously decorative spread is not something that you will lay out every time a few friends drop by for a drink! Not only does it take a great deal of time, but also the quantities of ingredients are such that these spreads are best suited to a cocktail party with many guests. In that case, however, it is well worth taking the time and trouble to set out the snacks in such an attractive and festive manner. Working out the various combinations of ingredients (shape, size, and color must be taken into account!) and arranging them into attractive patterns is not only fascinating work, it is also great fun! It is even more fun with a helper.

The most important thing is to make a

▲ This cheese dish is of somewhat more modest proportions than the spread opposite! The cheese blocks must be assembled directly on the serving tray. If this is done carefully, no further support is necessary. If you are in any doubt about the stability of the structure, simply use toothpicks to give additional support.

Crackers and French bread (see page 49) are served separately.

Dishes of snacks and ▶ tidbits form the gardens and orchards in this edible landscape, while the houses of the "landed estates" and the paths between the gardens are built of various crackers and toasts which sit loosely one on top of another. It is sensible to build the estate houses right on the serving table. The dishes and bowls of healthy snacks and ready-made salads can be prepared earlier and kept under plastic wrap in the refrigerator.

plan before you begin. Make sure that similar sorts of snacks are set out together and that all the ingredients are easily accessible. Also ensure that the plates, toothpicks, knives and forks, etc. are set out handily for your guests.

◀ First decide the approximate design of the estate houses and then begin building with a number of empty cracker boxes.

Stack the crackers and toasts in such a way that those perched at an angle rest against the cartons. The roofs consist of pieces of Swedish rye crisps or matzo laid flat or set at an angle.▼▼

◀ Empty the boxes the crackers came in, and use them to build up the houses and rooflines. Fasten these boxes together with adhesive tape.

◀ Attach double-sided adhesive tape to the bottom of the cartons, and fix them firmly to the serving table surface so that they won't move while you are placing the crackers and toasts.

The ingredients — "trees and plantings" — of the orchards and gardens are set in a thin layer of prepared salad, or they are sliced diagonally and set out in layers. ▶

▲ Because of the support provided by the cartons (which are attached to the surface of the table) the cracker and toast roofline is much more stable than it would appear at first, even though the elements are only loosely stacked. You can gain extra stability by not piling the toast and crackers too high and by inserting pieces of Swedish rye crisp to bind the elements together.

The empty spaces at ▲ the front of the board can be filled with small, prepackaged triangles of various soft cheeses.

◀ Place two circular paper or cardboard plates, and build the bottom layer of the cheese-block wall around the outside. Leave a space for the gateway arch. Lay the second layer staggered in the way a builder lays bricks (each piece lying over two pieces in the lower layer). This makes the wall much more stable. Fill in the space behind the semicircles so that the walls are supported continuously from the rear. Make sure that the cheese blocks are about the same size so that they fit together easily. When the walls have been built, garnish them with grapes and olive (see page 64), and then set the Brie in the semicircular alcoves.

# Let's face it — kids love it!

These Fun Food plates probably do not need any explanations; the faces speak for themselves!

◀ In place of the two frankfurters that form the mouth, you can use a second fish stick or even a thick curved strip of applesauce.

▼▼ A children's salad such as this (see photo, lower left) is a good dish to serve at a birthday party. Many variations are possible: You can leave out the tomato cheeks or use radishes or silver onions for the eyes. You can also make the nose from two peas, a piece of carrot or a small radish.

## Stuffed oranges

Clean the fruit thoroughly; cut them in half, and squeeze out the juice. You need 14 fl oz (4 dl) including the juice of 1 lemon. Add ⅜ oz (12 g) of gelatin (following the instructions on the package), and add 2 oz (60 g) of light brown sugar. Stir thoroughly.

Scrape out any remnants of pulp from the inner surface of the orange halves. Fill these with the liquid gelatin, and set them aside in the refrigerator to set. When they have set, pipe the faces in whipped cream, and garnish with canned mandarin oranges. ▼

They say that an apple a day keeps the doctor away, and so, perhaps do other fruits! But when it comes to creating Fun Food with fruit, certainly "variety is the spice of life." Sprinkle the apple and banana with lemon juice to prevent any discoloration. And to be on the safe side, warn the children that the plums contain pits! ▶

A clown pudding with fruit, whipped cream, and candy will bring a smile to any child's face! Add the raspberry eyes and candy nose at the last minute to prevent the colors blending. ▼ ▼

This slice of pound cake, decorated with various candies, is a colorful birthday treat. The face is set off by the myriad bright-colored sprinkles all around the outside. ▼

Mashed kale, cabbage▲ and potato, moulded and served with smoked sausage (a favorite winter dish in Holland, at least!), may appeal to even the most fussy child, when presented in this way.

Traditionally, a hollow "nose" is pressed in the surface and filled with gravy. If the children do not like onions, then instead use extra slices of sausage for the eyes.

▲▲ Slices of pineapple, whipped cream, canned mandarin oranges, two cherries or blueberries, and a strawberry are all the ingredients you need for this sad-looking clown's face dessert.

◄ A fish stick and mashed potato are combined with carrots and a couple of sprigs of parsley. The mashed potato hair is piped with a large star-motif decorating tube. (You can also use peas for the hair).

Pancakes almost insist ▲ on being decorated! Haven't we all felt the desire (and probably indulged it, too) to decorate a plain pancake with a spoonful of jelly or syrup? The simplest way is to fill a piping bag with jelly, and pipe the hair and mouth. Slices of kiwi fruit and a strawberry complete the "picture."

▲▲ Slice a small single-serving container of vanilla pudding in two and lay the halves next to each other (without the container) to form the eyes. Pipe the lower part of the face with whipped cream, and lay cherries to form the mouth. The hair is made of cherry jelly or cake filling.

◄ A breakfast we could all face! A fried egg, bacon, tomatoes, and a gherkin (or sausage).

71

◀ A juicy and healthy snack for a children's party . . . that's what these festive-looking oranges provide. And not only that, but the engraving in the skin also releases the aroma; they smell delicious!

It is best to work on a sheet of plastic since the skin contains orange pigment. Black soft-tipped-pen design markings can also stain a working surface.

A linoleum-block gouge is unsuitable for this since the skin is too soft and the fruit itself too small. There is also the risk that the gouge will slip and give you a nasty cut. Any minor mistakes in the cutting can be corrected easily with a fruit knife. Clean the knife frequently while you are working. Take care not to cut into the flesh as this reduces the period during which the fruit remains fresh.

# Peel engraving and fruit figures

Knives designed for ▲ engraving fruit and vegetables can be found in specialty shops. They are available both for the left-handed and right-handed person and come in different sizes that are intended for various types of fruit. To ensure that the engraved line is an even width and depth, rest the bottom of the blade directly on the fruit as you work (see photo, right).

Engraving is a pleasant and (depending on the subject) quick way of decorating fruit. Choose fruit that has a fairly thick rind so that there is little chance of damaging the flesh during engraving. That way the fruit remains fit for consumption. Another important condition is that the color of the rind must be different than that of the layer beneath it. The watermelon provides an optimum contrast — the dark green of the rind and the almost white flesh go beautifully together. Large oranges are best decorated with very simple patterns — a spiral from top to bottom (see photo, left); straight, curved, or zigzag lines; circles, stripes, or crosses.

## INGREDIENTS

- ○ 1 nicely shaped large, hard green water-melon
- ○ pineapple and/or melon
- ○ slices of strawberry
- ○ pitted cherries
- ○ piece of apple (with green peel)
- ○ slices of banana
- ○ juice of various fruits (press any unused pieces)

◀ These sharp linoleum-block gouges are highly suitable for engraving the smooth, hard skin of the green watermelon. The interchangeable gouges allow you to cut lines of various thick-nesses.

▲ To make the dish truly festive, fill it with a variety of chopped and sliced fruit — see the recipe above left or make up your own.

An artistically etched ▲ watermelon such as this makes an original gift to present your host and hostess at a barbecue or some similar event. The list of ingredients and the design can be

adapted to suit the taste of the person for whom the gift is meant. The melon on the right for example, was designed for someone who is in-terested in prehistoric art. In contrast, the other melon decorated with flowers was de-signed for a young girl's birthday; such a gift takes on a highly per-sonal touch when the name and birth date of the recipient are en-graved on it.

◀ If you are not particularly good at drawing or designing, look for an appropriate drawing or photograph in a book or magazine and simply make a tracing of it (see below).

The design engraved on the melon shown here is actually a combination of two illustrations from two different books about prehistoric art: a wounded bison (from the caves of Niaux in the French Dordogne) and a stylized hunter (from the Valltorta caves in Spain).

Trace the illustration from the book using a sheet of transparent drawing paper. Cut the figure out; decide where it must be positioned on the surface of the melon, and attach it with adhesive tape. Trace the outline with a soft-tipped pen. ▼

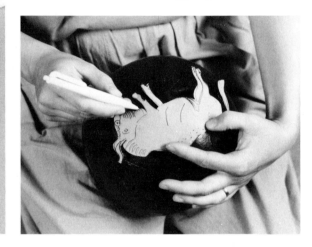

Larger fruits, particularly watermelons, lend themselves admirably to more complex designs, text, and even stylish drawings. This work involves much finer detail — you must frequently change the direction and thickness of the line and cut tight curves and angles — and therefore it is better to purchase a special set of linoleum-block gouges from your local hobby store (see photo page 73, left). Such gouges give you much greater freedom of expression in engraving work.

Whatever fruit you choose, make sure that they are large, firm, and regular in shape. Before starting work, clean the fruit, and polish it with a dry cloth. Draw the more complex patterns with a thin, water-resistant soft-tipped pen before you begin to engrave.

**Shelf life:** Engraved fruits remain fresh and edible for several days, as long as the flesh in not damaged. After a few hours, signs of drying out (discoloration, wrinkling) can be seen in and around the engraved lines. Although this looks unpleasant, the taste of the fruit is unaffected. This process can be delayed by wrapping the fruit in aluminum foil or plastic wrap.

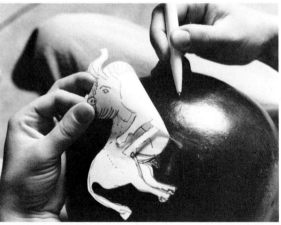

◀ After you have drawn the outline, draw in the interior lines. Do not remove the cutout figure from the melon, but leave it in place so that you can re-lay it to check the position of the lines. The easiest position to work for both drawing and cutting is simply to hold the melon on your knee.

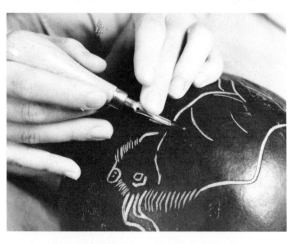

◀ Cut out the engraving with a linoleum-block knife. First cut the contours using a medium-fine gouge. Finer details (hair, eyes, mouth) are cut with a finer gouge. Hold the gouge in your "normal" hand, and guide it with the index and middle finger of the other. Keep your hand relaxed to ensure that the gouge doesn't slip.

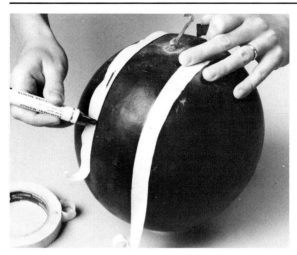

◀ 2. Draw a horizontal line around the melon about an inch (a few centimeters) above the middle. This is done by setting a soft-tipped pen on a can (or similar support) and turning the melon through 360°.

4. After the zigzag cuts have been made, cut the handle free with a large, sharp knife. Open the melon carefully. ▼

▲ 1. First determine the position in which the melon stays upright. If necessary, cut a thin slice from the underside so that the melon "basket" won't tend to lean over. Attach thin strips of adhesive tape to mark the position of the handle, and draw its outline using a water-resistant soft-tipped pen.

3. After the engrav-▶ ing has been completed, the melon is cut around the middle (except for the handle, of course) with a specially designed V-shaped knife. This should be held so that it is at right angles to the center of the melon and pushed firmly. Repeat this operation so that each cut touches or just crosses the adjacent cut.

5. Hollow out the melon using a large spoon so that the remaining wall is approximately ⅝ in (1½ cm) thick.▼

◀ Decorating knives can be bought in angular and rounded forms.

The birthday melon in its opened position, complete with filling.

Name and date of birth can be seen on the cut-out sections. ▼

This young character has the leaves from a bunch of carrots for hair. Of course, the apple still tastes the same, whatever the form of decoration! Cherries are much heavier than raisins, and therefore they must be fixed in place with toothpicks. Warn the eater beforehand, just to be on the safe side! ▼

▲ Cherries to make your mouth water — and when they are gone there's still the apple and the grapefruit to eat! The cherries, which form the "perm," are *not* mounted on toothpicks, so that the apple remains edible. Toothpicks are used, however, to fix the nose to the head and the head to the body.

The strawberry–cherry snails are ideal to use as decoration for a pie or a cake. They feel very much at home in a bed of whipped cream or a pool of fresh cream! You can find out how the snails are made on page 78. ▼

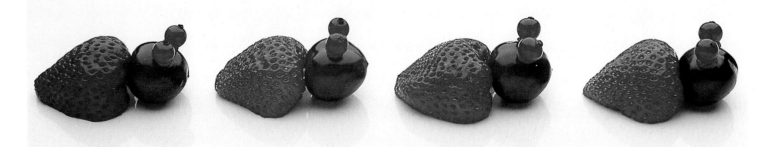

This banana-mobile ▶ racer can be made in almost no time. It should be made immediately before it is served; otherwise the banana turns brown. If the racer has to "come in for a pit stop" for a while, brush it with lemon juice. This model is very suitable as a treat at a kids' party. For a birthday party you can mount a candle to represent the "driver."

◀ Melon is a versatile fruit that can be used to create a variety of figures. This is especially true when it comes to making boats!

The figures are made from strawberries and cherries mounted on toothpicks, while the sail is "hoisted" on a long barbecue skewer.

The inside of the sail is cut into blocks, which can serve as "waves." You can also do this with a few strawberries, and then serve the whole tableau on a dessert dish.

Just watch the look on the children's faces when this ship appears over their horizon!

To make these barbecue ▶ sticks, cut the banana last, and sprinkle with lemon juice so that it does not discolor.

This little strawberry ▶ man, who is depicted almost life-sized, has a toothpick as his spine. This figure is just perfect for decorating a pie or pudding. Slice off the base of the strawberry so that the figure stands upright. The eyes are fixed in place with extra-thick, warm, water icing.

◄ Snip off the ends of the stems of the cherries to be mounted on the head. The stems should not be too short; otherwise the weight of the cherries will tend to pull them out of the holes in the apple.

◄ Prick a hole in the top of a firm apple. Preferably, use a green variety of apple as this gives a good color contrast. Push in the toothpick to about half or three-quarters of its length. Prick holes cherry by cherry so that you can position each one exactly. This way you also avoid making too many holes in the apple; this helps prevent it from going brown.

◄ Mount the nose in the apple. Warm the water icing a little; scoop a bit of it on a spoon, and dip the raisin (or currant) eyes into it. Press these against the apple, and hold them in place for a few seconds until they stick to the skin.

◄ When the head has been completed, place a toothpick in the apple for its neck support and position it over the middle of the grapefruit; mount it carefully. Make sure the two elements will still stand upright. If necessary, cut a thin slice from the underside of the grapefruit so that it is more difficult for the figure to tip sideways.

## An apple–cherry man

### EQUIPMENT

○ scissors
○ spoon
○ toothpicks

### INGREDIENTS

○ cherries
○ apple (green variety)
○ grapefruit or orange
○ thin carrot
○ raisins
○ confectioners' sugar
○ egg white

### INSTRUCTIONS

First wash and dry the fruit. Snip off the ends of the cherry stems, and remove the apple stem. Polish the apple once again with a dry cloth, and prick holes in the upper surface with a toothpick. Push the snipped-off stems of the cherries as deeply as possible into these holes. Set the nose in place using a broken piece of toothpick.

Make an extra-thick water icing (see page 11), and color it with a little cherry juice. Warm the icing in a saucepan, and use it to fix the raisin eyes in place (warming the icing ensures a better bond). Finally, mount the apple on the grapefruit, ensuring that the whole is well balanced.

## A strawberry–cherry snail

### INSTRUCTIONS

Cut off one side of the strawberry to make a flat surface for it to stand on. Remove the stem from the cherry, and fix this end of the cherry to the strawberry with water icing (see above). Attach the red currants *on top of* the cherry. The icing absorbs juices from the fruit and becomes soft after a few hours; if the currants are not right on top, they can easily fall off.

Cut a thin horizontal ▶ slice from the bottom of the melon segment so that the "boat" will be stable. This is particularly important for the sailboat because the sail is relatively heavy and tends to "capsize" the boat!

## EQUIPMENT

○ toothpicks
○ long wooden barbecue skewers
○ small paper (or plastic) flags and parasols
○ birthday candles

## INGREDIENTS

○ melon
○ dark cherries
○ strawberries
○ kiwi fruit
○ black grapes and/or cherries for the bar-becue skewers (see page 77)
○ lemon juice to prevent the slices of apple and banana from dis-coloring

Besides fixing the sail ▶ in place with a long bar-becue-skewer mast, use an extra toothpick to prevent it from turning. To mount the "crew" push the toothpicks through the strawberries so that they protrude a little at both ends. Stick one end into the melon, and mount a cherry on the other.

Handle the banana ▲ very carefully because this fruit will bruise and breaks easily. It is not necessary to slice a sec-tion from the underside — even though the ba-nana refuses to stand up-right! — since it will be up on its wheels. Instead push the toothpick axles through the fruit, and mount the kiwi fruit wheels. The banana-mobile racer now hap-pily stays upright on its racy green wheels! The "driver" is made in the same way as the sail-boat's crew.

Choose, for preference, a firm banana which is as straight as possible but which also has a distinct curve at one end (see photo left). The harder, slightly unripe, rather green bananas are best to work with.

# Cutout cakes in contrasting colors

Cut the two identical patterns from two different colored slices of cake. Swap the cutout patterns, and, presto, you have created these cutout cakes in contrasting colors! It couldn't be simpler, and yet the results are both attractive and surprising! Together with the children, you can quickly create decorated slices of cake for any number of special occasions. **Card cakes**, for example, featuring hearts, clubs, diamonds, and spades, make a perfect accompaniment to the coffee served during a bridge evening with your friends; a **football or soccer cake** goes down well while watching the game on TV; **mushroom cake** with a cup of hot chocolate is a fitting end to a long autumn country walk; and slices of **heart cake** (see page 81, top left) might well win the heart of a loved one when he or she comes to visit!

In short, with the necessary cookie cutter you can design similar slices of cake to suit almost any occasion.

## EQUIPMENT

- fairly small cookie cutters appropriate to the thickness of the cake
- flat, hog's hair pastry brush
- breadboard
- large teaspoon
- baking tin
- grill
- electric hand mixer
- scraper
- tablespoon

The small cutters used to make the "card-cakes" are bought in specialty shops. They are available in a wide variety of shapes and sizes and can be bought individually or in sets. The numerals 1 to 9, for example, form a set, and the letters of the alphabet can also be found as a set. However, these are so thin that often the cake falls apart as you try to push it out of the cutter.▼

▲ Have fun adapting the design of your cutout cakes to the occasion on which you intend to serve them. For example, the slices of "card-cake" above were specially prepared for a bridge evening. With a little imagination you can make similar cakes for other events.

## INGREDIENTS

If you intend to bake the cakes yourself, you may prefer purchasing packs of ready-prepared ingredients such as are available at supermarkets. You need two cake mixes — a dark (chocolate) and a light (vanilla). To prepare the cakes, of course, simply follow the instructions given on the packet; nothing could be simpler!

If you prefer to use separate ingredients rather than ready-made mixes, then you will need the following:

- eggs
- sugar
- butter
- self-rising flour
- salt
- vanilla
- cocoa (if necessary)

◀ Work, if possible, on two breadboards at the same time.

An electric slicer is not strictly necessary, but it will give you the best results when you cut the cake.

Ensure that the sharp edge of the cookie cutter is pointing downwards. This might seem to be gratuitous advice, but it is surprising how many first-time users inadvertently try cutting with the wrong end of the cutter! When the cutout shapes have been transferred to their new places and the slices are ready, lift them up carefully, one by one, and lay them gently on a serving dish or tray. If you pick up the slices with your hands there is a risk that they will break in two, especially if the shape is cut out close to the edge of the cake.

The best way to serve the cutout cake is to lay a sheet of waxed paper (or a paper doily) under each slice. You can serve them in small piles or individually on separate plates. The waxed paper not only supports the slices and prevents them from breaking, but it also means that the slices are easier to pick up and handle.

Of course, homemade cake is best! But if you are not in the mood for baking, then store-bought cake is a reasonably good substitute, although it may well be drier than homemade cake. Take extra care when cutting out the shapes and especially when pushing them out of the cutter. If you have difficulty finding plain cakes of suitably contrasting colors, you can substitute dark rye bread, spiced bread, gingerbread, or even ordinary whole wheat and white bread!

The most important thing, and this applies to almost all of the ideas described in this book, is that you use the examples as a basis from which to build your own imaginative and original creations.

**Preparation of the homemade cake:**

Because of the shapes to be cut out later, it is important that the cake be reasonably large. Measure the capacity of a high-sides baking pan, and adjust the quantity of the ingredients accordingly.

1 pint (½ litre) per baking pan capacity: 1 egg, 1¾ oz (50 g) sugar, 1¾ oz (50 g) butter, and 1¾ oz (50 g) self-rising flour. In addition, for a cake of normal size, you need ½ tsp. vanilla, and a good pinch of salt. Note: A cake of normal size is made in

▲ Ensure that the slice of cake is at least ¼ in (5 mm) thinner than the depth of the cookie cutter. Set the cutter in position, and press it down firmly through the cake. Lift the cutter with contents *vertically*, using both hands (see photo above). Do not cut too close to the edge of the cake.

Sets of cookie cutters on a particular subject are available in specialty shops and at good household stores. An example of this is the Christmas figures shown on page 114. These can also be used to make cutout cakes, especially as Christmas approaches!

a baking pan that measures about 9 to 11 in (24 to 28 cm) and has a capacity of approximately 6 pints (3 litres).

Cream the butter. Add the sugar, and beat until the mixture is smooth and light in color. Add the eggs, one by one, making sure the one is beaten thoroughly into the mixture before adding the next. Add the pinch of salt and the vanilla. Sieve the self-raising flour, and add it to the mixture; stir it through with a spatula. Do not mix further! Grease the baking pan with butter, and sprinkle it with flour. Fill it ⅔ full, and set in a prewarmed oven.

Baking time: about 75 minutes at 320°F (160°C), Marks ⅔. Put in the middle of the oven for gas; the bottom, for electric.

After baking, allow the cake to cool for 5 minutes before removing it from the pan. Bake your cakes the day before decorating them — the texture is then right. Make sure the slices are of equal thickness — though differences in thickness can sometimes give interesting effects! The slices should be ¼ in (5-mm) thinner than the depth of the cookie cutter to be used.

▲ The "contents" of the cutter should be pressed out gently (but firmly) and with even pressure, using the index fingers and thumbs. This is rather difficult with very small shapes; these can be pressed out using the handle of a spoon or the end of a pencil or brush. Great care is necessary in removing these cutout pieces, because small pieces crumble so easily, especially at the edges and ends.

▲ Broken bits of cake or large crumbs will sometimes remain stuck to the inside surface of the cookie cutter. This is particularly true with smaller cutters that have sharply angled corners. To achieve as sharp an edge as possible and an optimum contrast between the two colors, be sure to clean the cutters each time before they are used. To do this use a flat, hog's hair paintbrush. Double-check the cutters, especially the small ones, carefully for remnants of cake before cutting.

# Birthday treats for the whole class

◀ On a child's birthday why not present cupcakes with gum-ball heads to his or her classmates and teacher? These cakes are sturdy enough for a young child to hand them out in class without any risk of their falling apart! Prepare the cupcakes in plenty of time, because the egg-white icing needs 24 hours to harden.

Puff pastries filled ▶ with cream, smiling up at you . . . are delicious to eat, but vulnerable to damage on the journey to school and as they are handed out to classmates. These pastries are therefore better suited for older children.

Gum balls without ▲ cake can also make a festive gift. To give them more "body" these balls can be mounted on an egg-white icing base or on a cookie.

Use paper parasols here and there to set off the cupcakes. Chocolate éclairs (bought at the bakery) make a tasty substitute for puff pastries.▼

The cupcakes are not difficult to make, but the puff pastries require a little more experience and particularly patience. If you have no experience in making puff pastry, you can buy empty pastry cases from the baker, and fill them yourself. Another possibility is to make chocolate éclairs. With a little imagination you can apply "makeup" of cream, icing, or liquid chocolate to produce happy, smiling faces. A parasol completes the illusion of summer.

## INGREDIENTS FOR 12 PASTRY CASES

○ 7 fl oz (2 dl) water ○ 3 oz (90 g) butter ○ pinch of salt ○ 4 oz (120 g) flour ○ 4 eggs

It is most important that the ingredients be measured out as accurately as possible. If too much butter is used, the dough will not rise; and too much flour produces a flabby dough that will not hold its shape.

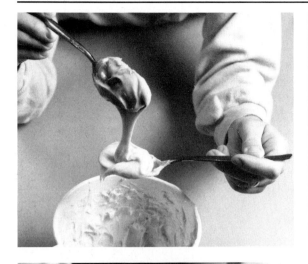

◀ By transferring the mix several times from one spoon to another, a homogeneous, rounded mass is created. This operation is very important; only when the mixture is spooned correctly will the puff pastries be successful. Practise as long as necessary before you finally spoon the ball of mixture onto the waxed-paper-covered baking tray (bottom left).

▲ Bake the pastries in the middle of a prewarmed oven for about 30 minutes at 390 to 440°F (200 to 225°C).

Make a hole in the middle of the underside, and fill the pastries with whipped cream.

The pastry can expand only so much as it is filled, so take care not to pipe too much whipped cream into it! ▼

Heat the chocolate icing,▶ and pour it into a bowl. Dip the puff pastries almost completely in the chocolate. Let any excess chocolate drain off, and set the pastry aside to cool on a tray or a sheet of aluminum foil.

## PREPARATION

Bring the butter, water, and salt to a boil. When the mixture boils take off the burner of hotplate and add the sieved flour directly. Whisk immediately, and continue whisking for several minutes until the mixture forms into a ball that comes loose from the pan.

Put the ball in a cold bowl, and leave to cool until the pastry dough feels lukewarm to the touch. Put it in a mixer, and add the eggs, one by one; mix until the dough takes on a glossy appearance.

Preheat the oven. Meanwhile cover a baking tray with a sheet of baking paper, and spoon out the pastry using two large tablespoons (see the photo series on page 86). The pastry balls should be as equal in size as possible and very shiny in appearance. The shinier the "skin," the more perfect the results will be.

Place the baking tray in the middle of the oven, and bake for 30 minutes at 390–440°F (200–225°C), Mark 4/5.

The pastries are ready when they are golden brown and feel light.

## EQUIPMENT

- paper cupcake moulds (these are available in various colors and designs)
- paper parasols
- flags on toothpicks
- piping bag with Ateco 2 (UK 2) tube
- star-motif tube

## INGREDIENTS

For approximately 20 cakes

- 10 oz (300 g) butter
- 10 oz (300 g) sugar
- 10 oz (300 g) self-rising flour
- 6 eggs
- a pinch of salt
- ½ tsp. vanilla
- 30 large gum balls
- 1 egg white
- confectioners' sugar

## INSTRUCTIONS

Separate the paper baking cups, being careful not to distort them in any way. Set them on a baking tray; about 20 should fit comfortably.

Fill the cups a little more than ⅓ full (no more, because then the cupcakes will rise above the edges and the finished figures will lose their "collars"). Place the baking tray in the middle of a prewarmed oven, and bake for about 30 minutes at 350°F (175°C), Mark 3.

The cakes are ready when they are golden brown and feel spongy to the touch.

To pipe the features warm the chocolate, and transfer it to a piping bag fitted with an Ateco 2 (UK 2) tube or a waxed-paper cone (see page 9). ▼

The "hair" of the puff pastry figure is piped with a largish, star-motif decorating tube. Use thick whipped cream for this. ▼▼

The gum ball is fixed to the top of the cupcake by a star-shaped dot of thick egg-white icing (see page 11). ▶

Twist the gum ball as you press it in place — this also twists the points of the star slightly to give an interesting effect.

Set the cakes aside for ▶ about 3 hours to allow the icing stars to dry, and then pipe the nose, mouth, and hair. Use an Ateco 2 (UK 2) tube for this. (See also pages 28–31). Set the cakes aside for at least 12 hours so the icing can harden.

# To celebrate a baby's birth . . .

◄ It is a custom in the Netherlands to mark the arrival of a baby by offering visitors rusks decorated with aniseed comfits. Presenting home-baked heart-shaped biscuits to the new mother instead is rather less traditional, but certainly more original! The typical white-pink colors of the comfits are echoed here in the decoration: pink comfits in white icing, and white comfits on pink icing.

Although pink is a very attractive color, it may well be that you prefer to celebrate the birth of a boy by making these biscuits in the traditional color of blue. White comfits on a light blue icing is quite lovely (see bottom left), but light blue comfits can't be found. Perhaps you will have more success! If not, a good compromise might be to pipe large dots in light blue icing instead.

◄ The pink of the aniseed comfits is a rather "hard" color compared with the soft baby-pink that results from adding red food coloring to the icing. To achieve a satisfying harmony between the two pinks, it is necessary to add a tiny touch of blue food coloring to the egg-white icing in addition to the red. This gives a lovely lilac-tinted pink, which is very close to the aniseed comfits.

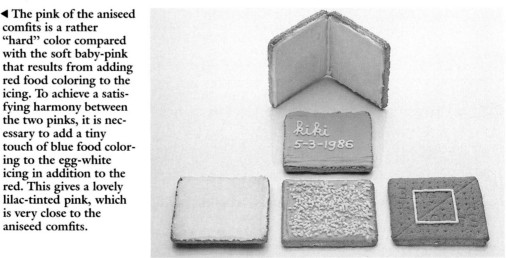

If you haven't had much ▶ experience at baking, or if you simply do not enjoy it, then this birthday-gift house can be prepared from rusks and cookies and other edible bits and pieces which you can buy ready-made in shops. The house of shortbread cookies or similar large biscuits is built around a pink candy "crib." If the new baby is a boy, then buy a blue crib and match the other bits and pieces accordingly. The dimensions of the house will vary according to the type of cookie you use, but they should be approximately 4½ × 3½ × 6¼ in (11 × 9 × 16 cm) in width, depth, and height, respectively. Smaller cookies can be

used, of course, but in that case the sizes of the decorations and the message must be adjusted accordingly.

▲ The house is built of 6 shortbread cookies, which are attached together with egg-white icing. Because ordinary aniseed comfits have such a strong color, in this instance it was decided to ice the base in pale pink icing and sprinkle it with white comfits instead of pink ones.

◀ The name and date of birth of the new baby can be piped onto the roof or one of the wide walls, as desired.

## EQUIPMENT

**For the birthday cookies:**

○ sieve
○ rolling pin
○ knitting needles, no. 5
○ cookie cutter(s)

**For the decoration:**

○ piping bag or plastic squeeze bottle
○ knife
○ tweezers

## INGREDIENTS

**For the shortbread pastry:**

○ 7 oz (200 g) flour
○ 5¼ oz (150 g) butter
○ 3½ oz (100 g) light brown sugar
○ a pinch of salt
○ vanilla

**For the decoration:**

○ 2 egg whites
○ confectioners' sugar
○ lemon juice
○ food coloring, red and blue
○ pink and white aniseed comfits

## WATER ICING

Since egg-white icing is thoroughly hard after a day or so, you might prefer to decorate these cookies with water icing, which stays much softer (see page 11). On the other hand, water icing always remains a little transparent, and thus the colors are not quite as beautiful. Furthermore, it is damaged more easily.

How the cookies or other homemade gifts are wrapped is of the utmost importance. A wide variety of lovely wrapping paper, boxes, bags, ribbons, and bows can be found at most good department stores and specialty shops. Look for something in silver, white, and/or pastel tints. Paper doilies and tulle also make excellent wrapping materials.▼

## PREPARATION

Sieve the flour, light brown sugar, vanilla, and salt together over a large mixing bowl. Take the butter from the refrigerator, and cut it into cubes. Add it to the flour mixture. Now knead this by hand to form a solid ball of dough.

Set this in the refrigerator for an hour to stiffen; it must be at the right temperature to roll out easily. If the dough is too warm (i.e., soft), then it will stick to the board and rolling pin. When it is too warm it is also difficult to "stretch," and the shapes you make will distort. When it is too cold (i.e., hard), it is difficult to work with.

Sprinkle your working surface with sieved flour so that the rolled cookies will not stick to it. Place the knitting needles approximately 8 in (20 cm) apart — the rolling pin must be able to roll over both of them at the same time. Place the ball of dough between the needles; rub flour on the rolling pin, and roll the dough out flat. Roll until the rolling pin glides smoothly over both of the knitting needles — the dough is then of even thickness.

Grease a baking tray or cover it with a sheet of baking paper, and lay it next to the rolled dough. Cut out the cookies, and lay them on the baking tray. Prewarm the oven to 300 to 350°F (150 to 175°C) (Mark 2/3). Place the baking tray in the middle of the oven, and bake for approximately 15 minutes. The cookies are ready when they are light brown. Leave them on the baking tray to cool. When they are cool, loosen them carefully from the tray with a spatula or some similar utensil. You can continue work when the cookies are cold.

## INSTRUCTIONS

Make a thickly fluid egg-white icing (see page 11). Bring half the icing to the required pink color by adding red food coloring. Add a few drops, stir well; check the color, and, if necessary, add a few more drops to get the desired color. Finally add a tiny drop of blue food coloring.

Use a plastic squeeze bottle or a piping bag to apply the icing to the cookies. First, pipe the outer contour a little less than ½ in (4 mm) from the edge, and then fill in the enclosed space (see photo, top left). The icing should flow into a smooth layer

▲ With adhesive tape attach two strips of thick cardboard, 5 in (12 cm) apart, to a sheet of paper. Pipe a thick strip of egg-white icing along one long edge of a cookie. Set both cookies against the cardboard strips, with the icing strip to the inside, and press them firmly but carefully together along the "ridge." If necessary, pipe a little additional icing along this ridge, and work it into the groove with a wetted finger. Let this dry for at least 6 hours.

Pipe the text in white▼ on the pink or light blue background. Fix the pieces together using a substantial quantity of egg-white icing. Let them dry. ▶

## EQUIPMENT

○ piping bag with Atero tube 2 (UK 2) or a plastic squeeze bottle
○ spatula
○ tweezers
○ paper, adhesive tape
○ cardboard strips

## INGREDIENTS

○ large shortbread cookies
○ sugar confectionery: flowers, hearts, birds, silver tablets, almond crib, etc.
○ 2 egg whites
○ confectioners' sugar
○ food coloring, red
○ aniseed comfits

by itself. If it does not do this, then smooth it out carefully with a wet knife.

Select the larger white and pink bead sprinkles, and place them in the icing layer, one cookie at a time, using tweezers.

The baby's birthplace is made in stages:

**1.** Prepare the egg-white icing. Mix a few drops of red food coloring into half of the icing to produce a light pink color. Use a spatula to spread white icing on one side of 4 cookies and pink icing on one side of 2 cookies. The icing layer should be approximately ⅛ in (2 to 3 mm) thick so that it covers the cookies adequately. Set one of the two pink cookies aside for a half hour to dry, and sprinkle the other white aniseed comfits. Press these carefully into the icing. The icing must be not too liquid in texture, or the aniseed absorbs moisture and becomes pink! Leave the cookie to dry for at least six hours. The icing still won't be very hard, but you can work on it further.

**2.** Take two white cookies, and set these against each other as shown in the top photo. The other two white cookies (the walls) are now given a coating of pink icing on their uncoated side. Finally, apply the text to the other pink-iced cookie using an Ateco tube 2 (UK 2) or a plastic squeeze bottle with a small opening. Clean the opening frequently with a paper towel (see page 23). Set aside to dry for at least 6 hours.

**3.** Use thick, white egg-white icing as mortar to attach first the back to the base and then to the two sides (pink icing outward). Don't be too sparing with the icing mortar. Press the pieces firmly together so that the icing squeezes out and fills any empty spaces. Set aside for 12 hours to dry.

**4.** Attach the roof to the sidewalls by means of two thick strips of egg-white icing. Set aside to dry for 12 hours.

**5.** Apply a thick layer of egg-white icing to both sides of the roof, and fix the decorations in position using tweezers. Pipe the windows on the sidewalls, and fix the flowers, the meringue "turrets", and the birds in place. Set aside to dry, for 24 hours, and your house is ready for occupation!

As you can see from the above instructions, making this little house does not demand a lot of time, but the work is spread over several days because of the in-between drying time required by the egg-white icing. Bear this in mind when preparing such a house for the new baby!

# Cookie decoration — from gingerbread men to gilded festive figures

## EQUIPMENT

- paper and cardboard
- colored pencils
- broad, flat brush
- disposable plastic cups
- teaspoon(s)
- piping bag with Ateco tube 2 (UK 2) or a plastic squeeze bottle

## INGREDIENTS

- gingerbread men
- egg whites
- food coloring
- confectioners' sugar
- silver candy beads, confectionery flowers, confetti, tiny bead sprinkles, etc.
- soft candy such as gum balls, licorice candies, etc.
- chocolate chips

In the Netherlands, Saint Nicholas distributes gifts to children on December 5. These beautifully decorated gingerbread men represent Saint Nick and his assistant Piet, and are traditionally eaten to celebrate this festival. Once upon a time such cookies were made and decorated by a local baker, but now families enjoy a creative evening at home decorating gingerbread figures themselves, which is much more fun! And you don't have to wait for Christmas, because such tasty figures can be made for other occasions. You may be able to purchase gingerbread moulds from a baker or a specialty shop. If you have difficulty finding them, then perhaps someone in your family — with a block of wood, a few simple tools, and a little imagination — might be able to design and carve a mould in which to press the dough before it is baked.

A few basic points: Children feel more at home with a short, broad figure than a long, thin one. Large models 12 in (30 cm) are easier to work with. If you buy the

Gingerbread figures can be bought in specialty shops. When buying check that the figures are undamaged. Carry them home carefully. These models are 11 and 15 in (28 and 38 cm), respectively.

◄ If available, you will undoubtedly prefer using flat stamp tweezers with rounded ends.

• 1. Take a sheet of white paper on which the gingerbread figure fits comfortably, and draw the outlines using a black soft-tipped pen. ▼

4. Lay down the fairly ▲ thin icing "paint" with a flat paintbrush. First set a large daub in the middle of an area, and then brush it out towards the relief lines.

2. Lay the figure next ► to the outline drawing, and draw in all the important relief lines "by eye." You are making a design sketch, and thus it doesn't matter if the positions of the lines are off by an eighth of an inch (a few millimetres).

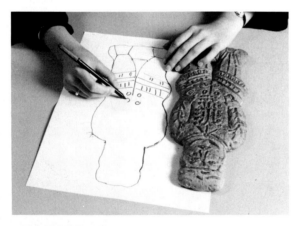

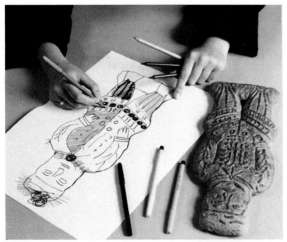

◄ 3. You can also color in the areas roughly, as long as the relief lines are still clearly visible. Use colored pencils, if possible, but soft-tipped pens can be used. Only use colors that can be produced with food coloring. After you have colored in the sketch, set the candy beads, flowers, and confetti by the sketch, and try them in various positions until you are satisfied that you have achieved the effect you want.

the figures, make sure there are no cracks in the surface and that the relief is complete and sharp. Finally, the figure should be thick and solid enough to handle safely.

## DECORATION

Although similar beautifully decorated cakes and cookies are often stored for long periods of time (sometimes they are not eaten at all), you must still bear in mind that the decoration should be edible.

The simplest and cheapest method is to decorate a gingerbread figure with sugar icing in various colors. Flat areas are painted, and lines are piped. Gold and silver bead sprinkles can be added here and there to give a more "lustrous" appearance. The end result will be something like the combined Saint Nicholas and Piet figure in the middle of the previous page. Of course, a much larger quantity of ready-made garnishing material — shiny balls, silver batons, small and large sugar flowers, single- and multi-colored bead sprinkles, and sugar confetti has been worked into the richly decorated figure on the right of page 93.

This method of decoration is too expensive for children to do as a school project. Nevertheless, using licorice candies sliced with a utility knife, peppermints, chopped gum balls, bead and chocolate sprinkles, excellent results can be achieved. When you are decorating in this way for the first time, a design sketch on a piece of paper can be a

**5.** Immediately after you have brushed on the icing, press the candy beads, batons, and flower in place using a pair of tweezers.

**6.** Now sprinkle the ▶ tiny bead candies, chocolate chips, and sugar confetti over the wet icing, and press them gently into place where necessary. Work area by area, and leave the figure to dry after each area is completed.

**7.** Certain areas of the figures can be built up with larger garnishing materials. This was done with the headdresses of the figures on pages 92 and 93. Always allow the icing sufficient time to dry and harden before continuing work in the same area. ▶

**8.** The final stage is to pipe the last fine lines using thick icing. While you are doing this, clean the tube frequently with a paper towel. ▼

welcome aid. First draw the outline and the main internal lines; then color in the figure. Keep the garnishings by you. The relief lines form the basic guide to the decoration and should be accented rather than hidden. When you are completely satisfied with the design, lay the gingerbread figure on a sheet of cardboard so that you can turn it around easily.

For painting the flat areas, make a thin confectioners' sugar icing, preferably with an egg-white base, but you can use water instead (for the recipes, see page 11). Use a broad, flat brush to apply the icing. The confetti, chocolate sprinkles, etc. should be sprinkled immediately onto the wet icing and pressed down gently. Leave this to dry for an hour, while you continue working on another area of the figure. Now turn the figure over, and shake off any excess garnishings. Take care that the garnishings do not come in contact with areas or lines that are still wet. Complete each area before moving on to the next.

When adding color to the icing, work in a logical manner: For example, first paint all of the light-pink areas; then add a little more red food coloring, and complete all the dark-pink areas. A little blue can then be added to make a violet/purple color, and those areas painted. Finally, add a little more blue and green to make brown. Green is created by mixing the leftovers of the blue and yellow icing together.

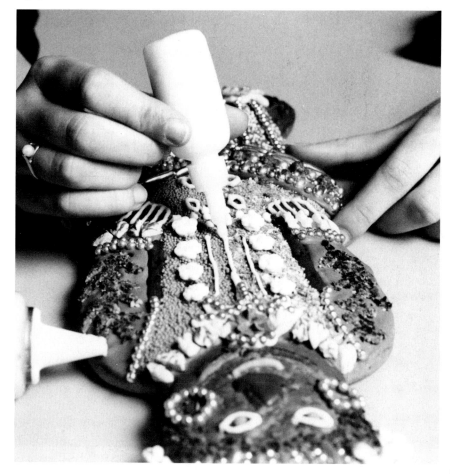

# Meringue, chocolate, and fondant: ingredients for a "sweet" Christmas Eve

These meringue goodies are intended to go with coffee during a pleasant, festive evening with family and friends. Preparation won't take up too much of your time — at least not if you've done this work before — and it isn't at all difficult. Simply pipe the figures on a baking tray in spare moments between packing Christmas gifts, and pop them in the oven. Meringue keeps for weeks when stored in a cookie tin, so you can quite easily make figures at convenient times in the weeks leading up to Christmas.

The chocolate letters and fondants are intended as extra-special personal gifts for a

▲ Individual and personalized chocolate letters or fondants intended as Valentine or Christmas gifts can be made quite quickly using ready-made sugar confetti and flowers.

The beautiful roses that decorate the fondant are made following the method described on pages 17 to 24.

▲ The steamboat is "baking pan size." After it is baked, the boat is mounted on a supporting template by means of egg-white icing and long pins. This operation should be carried out with care because the meringue is extremely fragile. Make a cardboard or Styrofoam support using the original paper template. Broken-off bits of meringue can be re-attached with egg-white icing. Set aside to dry for at least 18 hours.

▲ Christmas gifts to relish; the sizes vary from 4 × 4 in to 4 × 8 in (10 × 10 cm to 10 × 20 cm). Make them fairly thick and don't forget to add a little flavoring to the mixture. This figure measures approximately 3½ × 4¼ in (9 × 11 cm) — enough to provide a tasty bite! ▶

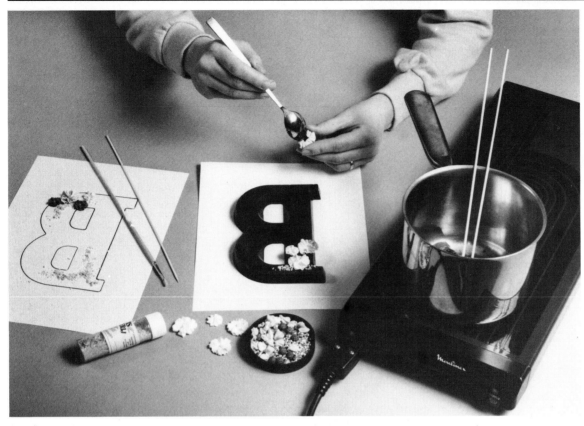

### EQUIPMENT

- long barbecue skewers
- tweezers
- heavy-bottomed metal saucepan
- teaspoon
- thin hog's hair brush
- hot plate
- paper
- piping bag
- paper doilies

### INGREDIENTS

- chocolate letters (plain chocolate sets the colors off best)
- fondant
- sugar flowers (bought or homemade)
- green sugar confetti (for the letter)
- tiny green bead sprinkles (for the fondant)
- egg whites
- confectioners' sugar
- food coloring, green

friend or family member. Of course, they can be eaten immediately, but they are usually displayed with the other gifts under the Christmas tree.

Pack the letter or fondant between paper doilies in a sturdy cardboard box. Lay a few crumpled sheets of tissue paper or crêpe paper on top. This method of packing helps prevent damage to the confectionery flowers.

◄ Cut a sheet of baking paper to the size of the baking pan. Fix it to your working surface with dots of meringue at the four corners.

Pipe the outline of the shape you wish to make (maximum size) 4 × 8 in (10 × 20 cm), and fill it in with a smooth, side-to-side movement.

### INSTRUCTIONS

Draw the outline of the chocolate letter on a sheet of paper, and place the flowers and other decorations within the contours. Move them about, trying out different patterns, until you are happy with the composition. Soften a thick strip of plain chocolate in a pan, but don't allow it to melt (see page 38). Transfer a little chocolate to the back of each flower, and gently press each in position on the letter. To make the leaves, brush a little chocolate thinly on the surface of the letter, and sprinkle sugar confetti.

The decorations for the fondant are attached in position with egg-white icing (see page 11). Begin with flowers, then pipe the stems; sprinkle tiny bead candies over, and finally pipe the text.

If you only have a small decorating tube, pipe a second layer of meringue over the first. The finished gift must not be too thin or it will be too fragile.

◄ Apply the ribbons and bow immediately after filling in the "box." Make sure that you achieve a good contrast in color, although this is rather difficult to see here (it is better seen in the photos on page 97).

Do not use too much food coloring as the figures tend to look less tasty!

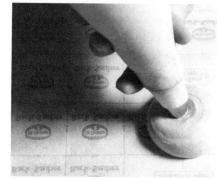

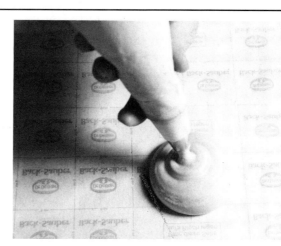

◀◀ When piping, first hold the mouth of the nozzle *within* the meringue mixture. When the ball has a diameter of approximately 2½ in (6 cm), lift the nozzle, and pull it quickly towards you to create a ◀pointed "nose."

## EQUIPMENT

- ○ mixer
- ○ bowl
- ○ piping bag
- ○ decorating tubes (large-format star motif, fine tube, and normal opening)
- ○ baking paper

## INGREDIENTS

- ○ egg whites
- ○ fine granulated sugar
- ○ food coloring
- ○ flavoring
- ○ silver candy beads
- ○ chocolate (icing)
- ○ tiny colored bead sprinkles

## PREPARATION

The correct mixing proportion is 1 egg white to 2 oz (60 g) of sugar. A good quantity to begin with is 6 egg whites and 12 oz (360 g) of sugar. The egg whites should be at room temperature so that the mixture stiffens more quickly. If necessary, place the bowl in a larger bowl of hot water while beating.

Put the egg whites in a bowl, and add a little sugar. Beat the mixture, adding the rest of the sugar as you do. Beat the mixture until it is fluffy and stiff. The mixture is ready if it remains in place when the bowl is turned upside down. Divide the meringue into the quantities you require, and add a few drops of food coloring and flavoring to each. Spoon this carefully through the fluffy mass. Ensure that there is absolutely no grease or fat on either your hands or your tools as the slightest trace will break down the meringue.

**Baking** takes place in a prewarmed oven at a temperature of 210 to 260°F (100 to 125°C). Actually, this process cannot really be referred to as "baking." Rather the meringue is dried and becomes lighter in weight and crispy in texture. Colors should barely change during this process.

During baking leave the oven door a fraction *open* so that moisture can escape easily. Baking time depends on the thickness of the meringue and varies between 1½ and 2 hours. The meringue is ready when it separates easily from the baking paper on its baking tray.

◀ After you have piped the light brown (flavored with mocha) meringue, take up the piping bag of light green meringue (see photo, page 97). If you only have one piping bag, then first pipe all that is light brown, and then wash the bag thoroughly in warm water. Dry the bag with a clean dish towel (watch out for any grease), and then begin with the next color. A star-motif tube is used for the green meringue.

◀ After the third color (yellow, with perhaps a taste of vanilla) continue with the colorless white meringue (with no extra flavoring). First pipe the collar using a star-motif tube. While piping make either a quick, short back-and-forth movement or a turning movement.

◀ Change the tube for the normal opening (large format), and pipe the bobble on the hat. Change the tube to a small-format normal opening. Pipe the eyes and mouth. If you wish, press silver candy beads into the eyes. Bake the meringue as described in the text, and set it aside to cool.

Use a very fine tube to pipe the eyebrows, nostrils, and the pupils of the eyes in chocolate.

# Marzipan for Christmas: perfect on a winter landscape cake

A fanciful landscape can very easily be created by combining different types of cake in varying sizes and shapes and pouring chocolate icing over the whole construction. Marzipan winter figures and confectioners' sugar "snow" complete this Christmas cake, which will be enjoyed by all the family.

Buy ready-made, uncolored marzipan at a candy or pastry shop. To make the figures illustrated on the right, you will need about 2 lbs (1 kilo). Do not allow the marzipan to come into contact with water. The "mortar" in this case is gin or other potable alcohol. When kneading in the food coloring, you must wash and dry your hands each time you begin a new color.

◄ The Santa Claus is about 3½ in (9 cm) high; the other figures are 2¾ to 3¼ in (7 to 8 cm). Use toothpicks to mount the figures on the cake. The colors should not be too vibrant.

The size of the *landscape cake* depends on the number of guests expected. This rather grand cake measures 16 × 14 × 10 in (40 × 35 × 25 cm) in width, depth, and height, respectively, but it can, of course, be smaller! ▶

◄ 1. The cake for the base is baked in a home-made mould made of waxed baking paper, folded to the size you require. A similar result can be achieved by slicing two regular cakes lengthwise.

4. Fill in holes and irregularities with bits of cake cut to size. ▶

◄ 2. You need: a base cake 16 × 12 × 1¼ in (40 × 30 × 3 cm); 2 turban-shaped cakes of 6¾ in (17 cm), one of 8¼ in (21 cm), and one of 9 in (23 cm) diameter; 1 large rectangular cake.

5. Brush an even layer of chocolate icing over the whole landscape. This can also be bought in packets which are put in hot water to soften. ▶

Note: For each approximately 17 fl oz (half litre) of mixture you need: 1 egg, 1¾ oz (50 g) each of butter, self-rising flour, and sugar.

For example: the home-made waxed-paper baking tray measures 16 × 12 × 1 in (40 × 30 × 2.5 cm), which is about 192 in³ (3000 cm³) or approx-

imately 6½ pints or 100 fl oz (3 litres); therefore about 6 times the quantities listed above are required. Instructions on preparing the cake mix can be found in the text on pages 82 and 83. Approximately 3 packs of chocolate mix are also required for icing the cake.

6. Soften blocks of chocolate (until they are just soft; melted but not liquid) on a hot plate (see page 38). Smooth out any holes, irregularities, and ridges. Set the landscape aside for several hours so the chocolate can set. ▶

▲ 3. Arrange the cakes on a marble or heavy wooden cutting board to form the mountain landscape. (It must be made directly on the cutting

board since it cannot be moved once the work has begun.) Make sure that the various cake elements are stable.

7. Finally, give the landscape another coat of chocolate icing. Allow it to cool, and then sprinkle it with confectioners' sugar. ▶

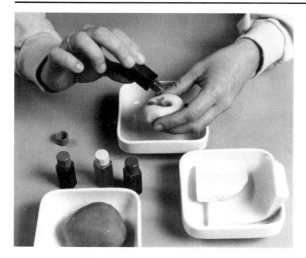

◄ Work over a bowl and color only a very small amount of marzipan: make a hollow in the middle, and pour in a few drops of food coloring; fold the hollow closed, and knead carefully.

Lay a template (see page 107) on a sheet of marzipan, and carefully cut out the holly leaf with a sharp, pointed knife. ▶

◄ 1. To make the body, mould a rectangular block measuring approximately 1⅛ × 1½ × ¾ in (3 × 4 × 2 cm). Cut diagonal lines inside the two longest sides (see photo left), and mould the arms.

A. Using the flat of your hand, roll out a cone from a ball of green marzipan. ▶

◄ 2. Form a square marzipan block 1⅛ × 1⅛ × ¾ in (3 × 3 × 2 cm). Mould the right and left legs by pressing a groove across the middle of the square surface. Make the shoes in the same manner.

B. Push the grooves into the sides of the cone using the handle of a knife, and mould it into a pyramid. ▶

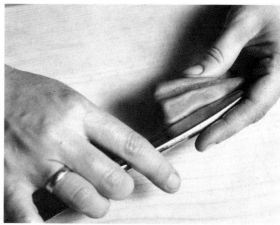

◄ 3. The two surfaces that must be attached are rubbed with gin (or another potable alcohol) and pushed in place. Small details (eyes, etc.) are pushed in place with the point of a toothpick.

C. Cut grooves at a ▶ slight angle along the side edges of the pyramid. From them mould the branches of the fir tree.

# Quickly decorated stylish Christmas cakes

Apart from the filling, the tart shown in the photo above is made entirely of meringue. A list of ingredients and instructions on how the meringue is prepared and baked can be found on page 99. For a tart like this you need 4 egg whites and 8 oz (240 g) of fine granulated sugar. As for the flavor, vanilla serves very well, and you can also add a little mocha (coffee essence) if you wish. Keep the color of the meringue neutral so that the colors of the filling are shown off to their best advantage.

The manner in which the case and lid are piped is shown on page 106.

Fill the case just before serving. The filling should not contain too much moisture as this causes the meringue to "melt." The case is substantial, but the lid is vulnerable. Store it flat, and take care that it is not damaged as you lay it down over the filling. If the lid is damaged, repair it with egg-white icing or thick, liquid chocolate.

▲ This tart has a diameter of 8 in (20 cm) and is intended as a dessert for 4 to 6 persons. It can be filled in various ways, such as with ice cream and/or fruit (sliced banana, kiwi, and strawberries, whole cherries, and pieces of pineapple). Top off this delicious dish with fresh whipped cream and/or hot chocolate sauce.

Sprinkling in or around a stencil or template is one way that you can decorate cakes and tarts quickly. Of course, you can let your imagination free in designing the templates. Certainly such decoration is not confined to Christmas cakes! ▶

◀ Cut out a circle 7 in (18 cm) in diameter from a sheet of drawing paper, and lay this under a piece of waxed baking paper fixed in place with dots of meringue. Pipe the outline of the lid with a large star-motif decorating tube, by following the circumference of the template visible through the paper. Pipe the dots so that they are touching. The piping is carried out in a slow movement, lifting the nozzle slowly as each dot is piped.

◀ Now pipe the "spokes," ensuring that the various elements touch each other. The spokes are formed by decreasing pressure on the piping bag as you move towards the middle while at the same time moving the bag more quickly. It is a good idea to try this out before you actually begin the real tart!

◀ The paper template is also used under the baking paper when you are making the flat base. This is piped by laying a closing spiral, starting from the outer edge of the template and moving steadily inward. Use a round, large-format tube. The base must be about ¾ in (2 cm) thick. If you are unable to get it this thick, pipe a second layer over the first.

◀ Build up the surrounding wall in ⅝ in (1½ cm) layers of meringue. The wall must not be higher than 1¾ to 2 in (4 to 5 cm). If you need a higher wall, then you should pipe a number of approximately ¾ in (2 cm) rings; bake them separately, and then mount them one on top of the other using egg-white icing as the mortar.

◀ Draw the template figures on heavy drawing paper, and cut out the areas that are to be covered with confectioners' sugar. Don't cut out fine details because too much sugar will fall on the surface as the template is removed, messing up the definition of the lines.

## PREPARATION

Prepare the cake following the recipe and directions given on page 26, with one addition: 2 tablespoons of cocoa powder are mixed into the flour before it is sieved. (This is to give the chocolate color and taste.)

## BUTTER CREAM INGREDIENTS

- 7 oz (200 g) butter
- 3½ oz (100 g) confectioners' sugar (sieved)
- ½ tsp. vanilla
- 2 tablespoons cocoa powder

For preparation see page 11.

◀◀ Spread brown butter cream carefully over the side of the cake. If this is too thin, then set the mixture in the refrigerator for a while before you use it.

◀ Press a handful of chocolate sprinkles into the butter cream on the side of the cake. Repeat this until the sides are completely covered with sprinkles.

◀ Sprinkle a thick layer of cocoa powder on the cake, and lay the template over it. Loose pieces of template can be positioned using long pins pushed no more than one-third of the way into the cake.

Sprinkle a thin, transparent layer of sieved confectioners' sugar over the entire surface, taking care not to hit the pins with the sieve.

▼ Transfer these template drawings to a sheet of white drawing paper by means of a sheet of carbon paper or tracing paper.

◀ Lift the templates vertically, being careful not to spill any sugar. Set any extra decorations in place using a pair of tweezers, taking care not to disturb the sugar patterns.

The cake should *not* be stored in the refrigerator. Be careful not to create a draft as you walk near or while carrying the cake, as this may disturb the sugar patterns.

# Santa Claus cake and shortbread Christmas trees

## EQUIPMENT

For the Santa Claus cake:

- baking mould
- paper clips
- spray to lubricate the baking mould
- sieve
- sprinkler for confectioners' sugar

## INGREDIENTS

- 3½ oz (100 g) each of sugar, butter, and flour (not self-rising flour)
- 2 eggs
- pinch of salt
- ½ tsp. vanilla

A confectioners' sugar ▲ sprinkler (with rotating sieve) is almost indispensable when you want to create a snow effect on cakes, tarts, pies, and even pancakes.

## PREPARATION

Beat the butter and sugar to a creamy consistency using a hand mixer. Add the eggs, one by one, mixing well. Sieve the flour, vanilla sugar, and salt into the mixture, and stir through with a spatula. Do not use self-rising flour under any circumstances as this gives a rough texture to the cake, which in turn affects the detailed shapes and reliefs of the Santa Claus figure.

◄ The baking mould must be greased thoroughly, ensuring that you reach every nook and cranny. The best way of accomplishing this is to use a lubricant aerosol spray that is widely available.

◄ To make a really lovely tree you need about five to seven cookie cutters. These can sometimes be bought in sets, but you can also collect them separately. The three smaller examples on the right are proper, closed cookie cutters. The larger trio on the left are actually designed for making fondant. This can be seen from the opening clip (left).

◄ Simple yet stylish, Santa Claus stands among the fir trees. Arrange the figures on a large tray, and generously sprinkle them with confectioners' sugar just before serving. The area around the trees can be filled up with cookies, chocolate holly leaves, etc.

Grease both parts of the baking mould evenly using an aerosol spray lubricant. Close the mould, and use extra paper clips so that it is completely closed all around.

Fill it ¾ full with the mixture. Tap the sides of the mould, and tap the whole mould on the working surface; push the mixture down with a spoon to ensure that there are no "gaps" between the mixture and the side of the mould.

Place at the *bottom* of a prewarmed oven, and bake for 25 minutes at 390°F (200°C), Mark 3. The cake should expand a little out of the mould. It is ready when it feels elastic to the touch.

Remove the mould from the oven, and

▲ Fill the baking mould ¾ full with mixture. Do this slowly so that the mixture can spread into the corners and so that any air bubbles arc eliminated. Press the mixture in with the back of a long spoon.

The delicacy of the texture of the baked cake determines how sharp the relief lines appear to be. Placing a candle next to the figure creates an attractive highlighting effect. ▶

set it aside for a few minutes to cool. Any excess cake protruding out of the mould is cut off using a sharp, serrated knife. Lay the mould flat, and remove the clips. Carefully remove the front section of the baking mould, and check that the cake is loosened from the back section. The cake should be removed from the mould only when it is completely cool.

**Finishing touches:** The figure is now sprinkled with confectioners' sugar. Should the cake be slightly damaged in places or if you are not satisfied that the relief is as good as it should be, then you can repair the cake using water icing poured and/or brushed in with a broad, soft brush (see page 94) or with egg-white icing piped with various decorating tubes (see pages 18 to 21).

▲ Similar three-dimensional moulds, actually meant for making chocolate figures, are available in various designs. In the photograph left you can see an Easter rabbit. You can even buy a mould of Santa Claus on horseback!

## PREPARING THE DOUGH

Sieve the flour and the granulated sugar, and put this in a bowl along with the vanilla and salt. Cut the firm butter into small cubes; add these to the bowl, and knead fiercely by hand until the ingredients form a solid mass that does not crumble.

Divide the dough into two rolls, and wrap it in aluminum foil. Leave it in the refrigerator for about an hour to allow it to stiffen. Do not allow it to become hard, however, as it then becomes too difficult to roll out.

Sprinkle your working surface with flour (by shaking it through the sieve), and roll

## EQUIPMENT

For the shortbread trees:

○ rolling pin
○ cookie cutters
○ aluminum foil

## INGREDIENTS

For 2 baking trays (approximately 2 trees):

○ 10 oz (300 g) flour
○ 7½ oz (225 g) butter
○ 5 oz (150 g) light brown sugar
○ pinch of salt
○ ½ tsp. vanilla

out the dough between two knitting needles ¼ in (7 mm) in diameter.

Cover a baking tray with a sheet of baking paper. Cut out the cookies, and lay them on the paper. Cut about twice as many small cookies as large ones, because the spaces between the larger cookies can be filled with smaller ones.

Place the baking tray in the middle of a prewarmed oven, and bake the cookies for 15 minutes at 300 to 350°F (150 to 175°C), gas Mark 2, until they are golden brown.

Remove the baking tray from the oven, and prick a hole in the middle of each cookie with a barbecue skewer. Loosen the cookies carefully from the baking paper using a spatula, and leave them to cool on a plate or some other flat surface.

◄ Immediately after the cookies are removed from the oven, and are therefore still warm and soft, a hole must be pricked in the middle of each using a sharp toothpick. Don't wait until the cookies have cooled, because they will likely break then, especially the small ones!

Make a stand for your Christmas trees from five 1¾ × 1¾ in (4 × 4 cm) squares of cardboard cut from the back of a notepad and a ◄ long barbecue skewer from which one point has been clipped. With a pencil, draw diagonals for each square. Where the lines cross is the middle. Prick a hole, smaller than the thickness of the barbecue skewer, at this point. Glue the squares together, using a needle to keep the holes aligned. When the glue has dried, mount this base on the barbecue skewer with a drop of glue. Sort the cookies into stacks by size, and build up the trees.

If a hole in a cookie has closed up while cooling, prick it with a toothpick (see photo) before you mount it.

◄ Begin at the bottom with 3 or 4 small cookies (see photo, page 110) and then continue as follows: one large cookie; two a little smaller; one smaller; one smaller still; one larger; etc. Simply stated, you want to vary the sizes so that the tree is as realistic as possible. Use smaller cookies as you near the top. Nip off the stick ¼ in (½ cm) above the next to last cookie, just before mounting the last one.

This diorama has a nice Christmas "feel" about it. It consists of large and small cookie cutouts. The house is 8 in (20 cm) high, the fir trees 8¾ in (22 cm). The Christmas tree just on the right is the same size. The Santa Claus above and the angel on the left are both 3¾ in (9 cm) tall. Present this diorama on a serving tray (set supports behind the cookies as shown on page 123).

Another method of presentation is to set the diorama out in a large, decorated cardboard box that has a rectangular hole cut in one end of it.

This gives a delightful "peep-show" effect.

Smaller figures can be hung on a Christmas tree.

## DIORAMA COOKIE FIGURES

The cutout cookies shown on page 112 are made with the same recipe as the star-shaped cookies on page 111.

They can be decorated entirely from your own imagination! First make a design on a sheet of paper; trace the cutout shape, and fill it in with lines and areas of color. Make several designs for each figure; choose the one you like best, and execute it on the cookies with water or egg-white icing. Whenever possible, avoid overlapping the layers, as there is always an in-between drying period of approximately 8 hours. If the cookies are to be eaten shortly after they have been decorated, then the drying time can be considerably shorter since the different colored icings won't have time to absorb each other's colors. Water icing is used exclusively for the figures shown on page 112. Icing for the

larger areas should not be too thick (a syrupy consistency) so that the layer flows out to form the outline (stay about ¼ in, 5 mm, from the edge), and then the inner area. The lines are piped with a plastic squeeze bottle or a piping bag with an Ateco tube 2 or 4 (UK 2 or 3), and for these the icing must be much thicker. Straight lines are made by setting the piece of work parallel to the edge of the table and allowing your wrist or the side of your hand to slide along this edge.

Sugar sprinkles, candy beads, chocolate buttons, or other "additions" should be set into the icing while it is still wet (see pages 92–95).

If something goes wrong, or is not to your liking, then scrape the icing off the cookie with an ordinary blunt knife, and start again.

If you intend to hang small figures on the Christmas tree, then don't forget that you need holes to hang them by. These should be pricked immediately after baking while the cookies are still warm. Make sure you do not cover the holes with icing! Don't leave decorating to the last moment; and if you do not have much experience, make a "trial run" a week or so beforehand.

When decorating the figures, especially the larger ones, do not apply the various colored icings in an impromptu manner. It is better to make a design on paper first. By varying the colors, lines, or shapes, you can make a large number of different cookie figures with one cookie cutter! ▼

▲ Small cutters can be bought in sets that come shrink-wrapped or packed in a box or a can. Larger cutters like those on the right that are 8 in (20 cm) high are bought separately.

Together with the "classic" Christmas shapes, other figures (in this case, animals) also look rather well among the greenery!

◀ These are shown "life-size" on the left. Trace the figures, and cut them out; then use them as templates to cut the dough.

After baking, find where the hole must be positioned: this is a little above the center of gravity, which you find by pricking a pin into the back of the cookie in various places until you find the point where it hangs straight down. Push a needle and thread through the cookie a few millimetres above this point. The professional way of making holes is to use a minidrill like that used by glass engravers. If you do this, then hold the drill vertically, and set another cookie under the first as a support. This stops the cookie from crumbling as the drill point breaks through.

▲ Pipe the meringue Christmas tree decorations to suit your own taste and imagination. They should not be too small (4 × 4 in, 10 × 10 cm).

Don't forget to add a few drops of food coloring to the meringue mixture.

See pages 98, 99, and 106 for the recipe, preparation, and instructions.

Hang meringue, like the cookies, on black thread. Prick the needle and thread from the back to the front, not too close to the edge. Do this while the figure is lying flat, and take great care because meringue breaks very easily. Ensure that the thread does not cut the meringue as you pull it through. ▼

▲ Kids are crazy about these mouth-watering candy gingerbread houses. The candies come off easily, while the gingerbread stays edible for weeks.

Here are the elements of the house. The straight lines have not been deformed during baking so that the elements are easy to attach together with egg-white icing. ▶

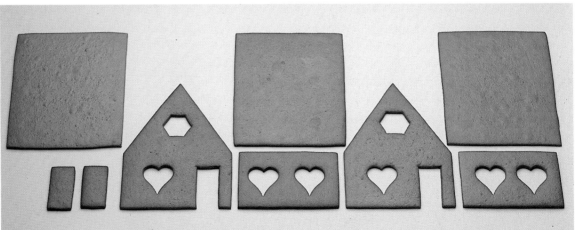

# Candy house and spiced gingerbread manger

## EQUIPMENT

Preparation and construction of the house:

- ○ extra-large bowl
- ○ long rolling pin
- ○ ¼-in (7mm) dowels, 18 in (45 cm) length
- ○ waxed baking paper
- ○ adhesive tape
- ○ aluminum foil
- ○ thin cardboard
- ○ ruler
- ○ utility knife
- ○ ordinary knife, not too sharp
- ○ cookie cutters
- ○ plastic-headed pins
- ○ paper clips
- ○ piping bag or plastic squeeze bottle
- ○ plastic-coated cutting board, 12 × 20 in (30 × 40 cm)

## INGREDIENTS

For gingerbread dough for the house approximately 7 × 7 × 9½ in (17 × 17 × 24 cm), length by width by height, illustrated left.

- ○ 1½ lb (750 g) honey
- ○ ¾ lb (375 g) granulated sugar
- ○ ¾ lb (375 g) vegetable shortening
- ○ 3 lb (1500 g) flour
- ○ 2½ oz (75 g) cocoa powder
- ○ 1½ Tbs cinnamon
- ○ 1½ Tbs gingerbread spice
- ○ 1½ Tbs ground cloves
- ○ 3 eggs

For the garnishing:

- ○ egg-white icing made from two large eggs (see page 11)
- ○ candies, almonds, pastry rings, chocolates, silver candy beads, etc.

## PREPARATION

Add the honey, granulated sugar, and the vegetable shortening to a heavy-based casserole, and cook until the sugar dissolves.

Set the mixture aside to cool. Sieve the flour, cocoa, and spices into a large mixing bowl, and add the cool honey mixture and the eggs. Knead fiercely with the hands to create a supple dough that is, and remains,

The candies can either be positioned in a random manner or according to a planned design and color sequence: e.g., red–pink–white. ▼

◄ First make a model in thin cardboard. When you are happy with the result, cut the model into separate elements, and use them as templates to mark out and cut the dough.

The photo on the right shows the house assembled, but not yet decorated. The base measures about 7 × 7 in (17 × 17 cm) and the ridge is 9½ in (24 cm) high. ▶

◄ Fix a sheet of baking paper to a flat working surface with adhesive tape, and roll out the gingerbread dough between two lengths of dowel, ¼-in (7-mm) in diameter.

Do *not sprinkle* flour on the baking paper to prevent the dough from sticking to it, and do *not rub* flour onto the rolling pin as this can create white areas after the dough has been baked.

If possible, have someone assist you by holding the dowels in place.

Use the grid on the left to enlarge the patterns to the required size. The squares are actually meant to be ⅝ × ⅝ in (1.5 × 1.5 cm) for the full-size templates.

Draw the outline square by square on thin cardboard, and cut out the templates: part A, two times (front and rear facades); part B, two times (side walls); and part C, three times (the base and two roof sections). ▼

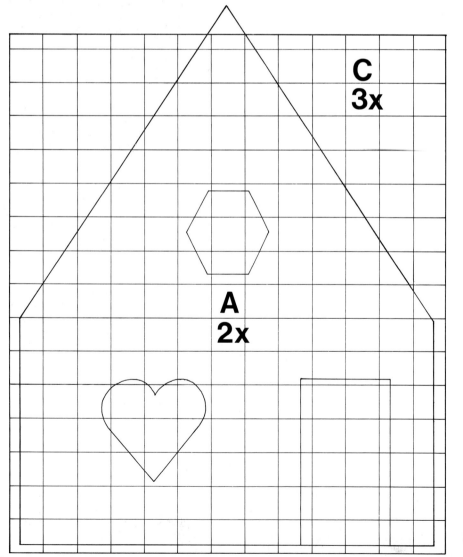

**C**
**3x**

**A**
**2x**

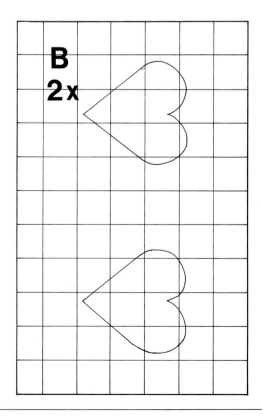

**B**
**2x**

very heavy and tough. Leave it to stiffen in the refrigerator for several hours. If you wish to keep the dough for several days so that you can make and mount the various elements in stages, then divide it into thick "ropes"; wrap it in aluminum foil or plastic wrap, and store in the refrigerator.

The dough must be rolled out on waxed paper as soon as it is removed from the refrigerator. If you wait too long, the dough becomes too soft and easily deforms as it is cut to shape. If possible work at a table that is accessible from two sides. Roll out the dough between two lengths of ¼-in (7-mm) wooden dowel. Continue to roll until the rolling pin glides over the dowels. This chore can best be carried out by two; one to roll out, and one to hold the dowels in position. Make sure that the rolling pin does not slip off the dowels as this can result in the dough being too thin in places. When the dough is rolled out to such a degree that the rolling pin will no longer straddle the dowels, cut a narrow strip off both sides. Roll with even pressure so that the dough remains flat, and ensure that no bubbles get underneath. Attach the corners and sides of the baking paper on which the dough is rolled firmly to the working surface with adhesive tape.

Cut out the shapes as soon as a sheet has been rolled out and before you begin to roll out another.

Lay a sheet of aluminum foil, mat side upward, on your work surface, and transfer the rolled dough to it in one quick, supple movement. If the sheet is particularly large (that for the roof or the base, for example), this transfer can best be carried out by two, one at each side of the table. Ensure that no bubbles get beneath the sheet. If this happens, prick a hole through the dough, and smooth it out carefully with a dry finger, using the minimum of pressure.

As soon as possible lay the cardboard template on the dough; make very shallow grooves around the outlines with a fairly blunt knife; remove the template; and with the same knife cut the lines through to the aluminum foil, taking great care not to damage the foil itself. You can avoid any chance of the cardboard sticking to the dough simply by smearing a little butter on the dough surface. If the cardboard still tends to stick to the greased surface, wrap it in aluminum foil. After you have drawn the lines, open the foil; remove the cardboard template, and gently and slowly peel the foil from the surface of the dough.

◄ Cut out the shapes with a rather blunt knife, being careful not to damage the aluminum foil.

If the template sticks to the pastry, then wrap it in foil. Return the discarded pieces immediately to the rest of the pastry dough, and knead it well, before rolling out the next sheet.

◄ Check that both the inside and the outside of the cookie cutter are absolutely clean. Place it in position, and press down firmly. Don't immediately remove the cookie cutter, but first remove the dough inside, holding the cutter in place with your other hand. Then lift the cookie cutter gently up and away from the dough.

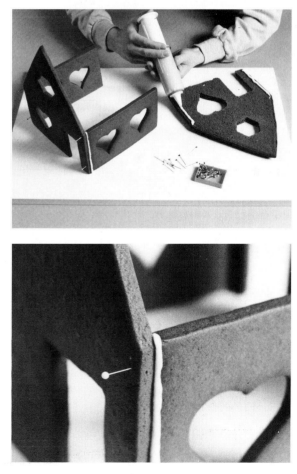

◄ Attach the facades and side walls together with a thick egg-white icing (see page 11). Apply the icing thickly using a piping bag or a plastic squeezer. Assembly takes place in various stages. First the front, back, and side walls are mounted, and then the assembly is set aside for 24 hours to dry. The assembly is then attached to the base, and the two roof elements placed in position. Again set this aside for 24 hours to dry before continuing work.

◄ Press the parts firmly together so that the icing is squeezed out, filling any gaps. The separate elements are held in position with plastic-headed pins, pushed in at right angles. Leave these in place until the icing has dried. Do not push the pins in completely, or they will be difficult to remove.

Cut the aluminum foil around the cutout gingerbread shapes, leaving an edge of about ¾ in (2 cm) all around. Put the shapes, on the aluminum foil, on a baking tray in the middle of a prewarmed oven.

Electric oven: 410–440°F (210–225°C), gas Mark 3–4. Baking time 20–25 minutes, depending on the thickness. If you have never worked with gingerbread dough before, it is better to experiment first,

particularly in regard to the baking time. After it has been baked, the gingerbread should be a lovely brown color, but it must not be too dark. When it comes out of the oven it is still quite soft, and the advantage of this is that it can easily be cut and trimmed off if it has lost its shape in any way: This, however, is not the intention. The cut shapes can, at most, be a few millimetres bigger than they should be, but straight lines must not be deformed in any way (see examples on page 116).

Leave the shapes on the baking tray to cool; then remove the aluminum foil.

## INSTRUCTIONS

In principle the methods of building the house and the Christmas manger are the

The gingerbread house is decorated and ready for Christmas! These (more expensive) Christmas chocolates, garlands, fir trees, and holly leaves give a more "adult" appearance to the finished house.▼

If you feel that the preparation and baking of such a gingerbread house is really too much work, then you can make one from bought spiced or gingerbread biscuits (see pages 88–91).

Three-dimensional gingerbread figures are difficult to make because the thicker solid parts distort and collapse during baking. Baking two layers, one on top of another, is possible as long as the layers are not more than about ⅛ to ¼ in (4 to 6 mm) thick. The figures in the stable were made like this. ▶

same. In fact, because the elements of the house are set at right angles to each other, building it is somewhat easier. The house is also sturdier, because it has four walls; this is also noticeable when building it. Read and study the text and photos on page 119. The gingerbread parts must be fixed together with sufficient quantities of eggwhite icing. Use long, plastic-headed pins to hold the parts together while the icing dries.

If this proves insufficient support (for the walls of the manger, which are set at an angle, for example), opened paper clips can be used instead of pins (see page 123, bottom right).

Although the house is completed before decoration begins, the Christmas manger is more complicated. The half almonds and glacé cherries are pressed into the dough before it is baked. Do not push them in too deeply, or you may deform the edge of the dough. A slightly raised relief should be visible around the almonds and cherries, however. If you wish, you can also add ⅛-in (3-mm)-thick stars and other Christmas symbols. When these have been cut and mounted, round off their edges by rubbing them with a dry finger. The dough, complete with almonds and cherries, is then baked in the oven. When they are ready, set the parts of the manger aside to cool, and then remove the aluminum foil. The mo-

◄ Unlike the house, the manger is not covered all over with candies. Of course, if you prefer this decoration, then feel free! But, to keep the style harmonious, only use Christmas chocolates (see adjacent pages left), and attach these only to the outer walls before you pipe the icicles.

Notice how deep the almonds and glacé cherries are pressed in before baking.

▲ The dimensions of the manger are approximately 12½ (w) × 6¼ (d) × 8 (h) in (32 × 16 × 21 cm). Make all of the elements from ¼-in (7-mm) thick dough, except for the middle wall, which should be ⅜-in (10-mm) thick. Cut the windows in the sides with a half-moon cutter.

Note that the decoration is on the inside. To make the fences lay strips of dough crosswise over each other. Don't bake them too long or they will turn black!

# CHRISTMAS MANGER

## INGREDIENTS

○ 2 lb (1000 g) honey
○ 1 lb (500 g) granu-
  lated sugar
○ 1 lb (500 g) vegetable
  shortening
○ 4 lb (2000 g) flour
○ 3½ oz (100 g) cocoa
○ 2 Tbs cinnamon
○ 2 Tbs gingerbread
  spices
○ 2 Tbs ground cloves
○ 4 eggs
○ halved almonds
○ glacé cherries

Each square is actually
meant to be ⅝ × ⅝ in
(1.5 × 1.5 cm) for the
full-size templates. The
manger is built up from
the following elements:

A. rear wall (1x) ¼-in
   (7-mm) thick
B. side walls (2x) ¼-in
   (7-mm) thick
C. roof elements (2x)
   ¼-in (7-mm) thick
D. middle wall (1x) ⅜-
   in (10-mm) thick,
   rolled out between
   ⅜-in (10-mm)
   dowels, baked a little
   longer
F. gable (1x) ¼-in (7-
   mm) thick
G. base (1x). Cut the
   trapezoidal shape
   from ⅜-in (10-mm)
   dough and roll it out
   in a free oval shape.

The fir trees and their
supports, the fence, and
the base layer (body out-
lines) of the figures are
cut from ¼-in (7-mm)
dough. The upper layers
(hair, arms, etc.) of the
Joseph and Mary figures
are cut from ⅛-in (4-
mm) dough.

ment to begin "construction," however, has not arrived!

The tiny dots around the almond and cherry stars must first be piped using a piping bag and an Ateco tube 2 (UK 2) or a plastic squeeze bottle. In either case, clean the mouth frequently. Pipe tiny stars, each consisting of three dots of icing, along the top of the inside walls. Leave to dry for 24 hours before beginning building.

The building of both the house and the manger takes place in two stages. **The house:** first fix the side walls between the front and back walls. Leave to dry for 24 hours. Fix the walls to the base, and set the two halves of the roof in place. **Christmas manger:** first fix the two diagonal side walls to the back wall, and fix the middle wall in place. Leave to dry for 24 hours. Fix the walls to the base with plenty of egg-white icing, and set the two halves of the roof in place (fixed in place with pins), after you have removed the paper clips from the tops of the walls. Mount the triangle under the ridge. Where necessary, run icing into the corners and grooves with a wetted finger. This helps to promote a good bond between the parts. Set the fence and trees in place with icing. If necessary, support them with toothpicks or pins. Leave the whole to dry for 24 hours, and then continue work.

**Decorating the house:** Of course, it is not necessary to decorate the house quite so extravagantly as that in the photo on page 116! The candies do not need to be close together (see photo page 120), and it is better if at least some of the gingerbread remains visible! Set the candies in place with egg-white icing. Don't use too much, or the candies will slip out of position. Heavy candies should be supported with a pin placed below them. Allow your imagination to run free, and don't try to be too exact!

**Decorating the manger:** The manger is decorated exclusively with egg-white icing and shaved almonds (browned in the oven). Apply the icicles using a piping bag with an Ateco tube 4 (UK 3). Begin just on the roof, and bring the icing slowly down over the edge, increasing speed as you do so to form a point. Making icicles is a matter of practice.

When the work is completed, leave the house and manger to dry for 24 hours before moving them.

If, like Joseph and ▶ Mary, the trees are free-standing, support them from behind with a right-angled triangle of gingerbread.

The arms and hair of ▲ Mary and the feet, arms, and round face of Joseph are made by laying a ⅛-in (4-mm) layer of dough over the first ¼-in (7-mm) layer. The contours round themselves off during baking. The crib consists of three parts: an oval-shaped base, a cylindrical body, and a small ball for the head. In the baking process all the parts meld together to form a homogeneous whole.

◀ After baking, apply the stippled decorations in egg-white icing. After allowing 24 hours for drying, assemble the manger in two stages.

◀ In certain places it is not possible to hold the parts together with plastic-headed pins during the drying process of the icing mortar. The parts can be fastened with an opened paper clip. The holes should be pricked out first with a pin.

# "Round the clock" salads for New Year's Eve

◄ This "mouse garden" salad, served on a tray measuring 13 × 17 in (33 × 43 cm), is enough for 6 to 8 persons.

Make sure that there is sufficient relief between the "hills" and the "lower ground." Push the long-stemmed broccoli "trees" into the higher salad landscape. The parsley "bush" is placed on the lower ground.

The trees can also be made from hollow stems of chives with parsley stems pushed into them (see page 47, third photo down).

If the salad is too soft to carry the weight of the cucumber "huts," cut a second piece of cucumber, a little shorter than the height of the "hill." Push this piece into the salad, and set the hut on top of it, if necessary with the aid of a toothpick. Finely chopped carrots, gherkins, or hard-boiled eggs can be used instead of peas to form the "stream."

A salad clock, which ▲ serves 6 to 8 persons, is a fitting dish to serve on New Year's Eve. Try not to make the mistake we did when setting the carrot numbers in position . . . Let's begin the New Year in the right way — or at least the right way around!

◄ The fact that attractive festive salads can also be made in single portions is demonstrated by this dish of the "mouse stranded on a forgotten island." The 8 peas play an important role in the composition, but they can be replaced by short lengths of chives or by three or four cocktail onions.

## INGREDIENTS

For a salad for 6 to 8 persons you need approximately:

○ 2 tins pink salmon
○ 10 firm tomatoes
○ 10 hard-boiled eggs
○ 5 Tbs silver onions
○ 6 to 8 medium-sized gherkins
○ 2 lb (1 kilo) potatoes (cooked)
○ 8 oz (250 g) peas
○ 2 to 4 Tbs salad dressing
○ mayonnaise
○ 1 head of lettuce

Roughly mash the cold potatoes, and place them in a large mixing bowl. Mash 6 eggs finely with a fork, and mix them into the potatoes. Chop the gherkins and silver onions finely, and mix them into the egg–potato mixture.

Clean and finely mash the salmon with a knife and fork, and stir through the mixture. Finely chop 4 or 5 tomatoes, and stir them through the mixture. Also add the pips and the juice of the tomatoes. If the mixture is not creamy enough add a few tablespoons of salad dressing. Stir peas into the mixture, making sure that they are not mashed in the process!

Leave the salad for 6 to 10 hours in a closed container in the refrigerator before garnishing it. (Prepare it the day before serving.)

◄ Make the clock salad directly on a circular serving dish (with a diameter of about 16 in, 40 cm). Wash the lettuce leaves, and dry them in a salad dryer or between two dish or paper towels. Set the leaves around the edge of the dish as shown in the photo, left. Spread the dark and light leaves equally.

◄ Take a cake mould about 9½ in (24 cm) in diameter and grease the inside with mayonnaise. Place the mould in the middle of the serving dish, and fill it with salad mixture. Push the salad down firmly, and smooth it with the back of a large spoon. Carefully remove the mould, and coat the top and sides with a layer of mayonnaise.

◄ If the salad mixture is a little on the thin side, or if you want the dish to appear a little bigger, round off the sides after you have removed the mould. Then apply the mayonnaise coating, and add the carrot or cucumber numbers and the clock hand. Press half-eggs and segments of tomato at equal intervals around the edge of the salad. Sprinkle the eggs with dried herbs.